6 MINUTE MORNING WORKOUT

6 MINUTE MORNING WORKOUT

FAYE ROWE & SARA ROSE

PaRragon

Bath · New York · Singapore · Hong Kong · Cologne · Delhi · Melbourne

First published in 2007

Parragon
Queen Street House
4 Queen Street
Bath BA1 1HE, UK

ISBN: 978-1-4075-0754-5

Printed in China

Produced by the Bridgewater Book Company Ltd.

Photography: Ian Parsons
Models: Samantha Fuery, Jade, Louisa Jarvis and Lucinda Jarvis

The publisher would like to thank the following for permission to reproduce
copyright material: Ken Chernus/Taxi/Getty: 13; White Cross Productions/
Photographer's Choice/Getty: 17; iStockphoto: 21 (top right), 81 (bottom
right), 121 (top left) and 157 (bottom right); and Jupiter Images: 39.

Caution
Please check with your doctor/therapist before attempting these workouts,
particularly if you are suffering from an injury, are pregnant or have just
had a baby. It is recommended that new mothers wait at least six weeks
post partum before participating in exercise (12 weeks if it was a Caesarean
birth). If you feel any pain or discomfort at any point, please stop exercising
immediately and seek medical advice.

CONTENTS

warm up/cool down

CONTENTS

stretching

CONTENTS

body toning

CONTENTS

flat stomach

CONTENTS

hips and thighs

Keeping your body in tip-top condition doesn't have to mean spending hours in the gym. Just 6 minutes each morning, in the comfort of your own home, is all you need to keep yourself in shape.

introduction

Six minutes in the morning – it doesn't sound like a lot, but spending just 6 minutes each day working out is enough to turn you into a fitter, healthier person. If you want a toned body, flat stomach, well-shaped hips and thighs and flexible limbs without spending hours in the gym, this is the book for you. It's ideal for beginners, so the exercises won't come as a shock to the system.

No doubt you've picked up this book because you're finding it hard to make time for exercise. It's no surprise, considering the busy lifestyles most people lead these days, that your health gets shifted to the bottom of your 'to do' list. The soaring cost of a gym membership, added to the fact that not many people have a gym on their doorstep (let alone one that doesn't cost the earth), means that the fitness-conscious among us are waking up to the idea of getting fit at home. The great thing about this book is that it covers such a wide range of exercises – and each section is easy to follow and fun to do.

As well as targeting your trouble zones, the stretching and toning sections offer an all-over makeover. So, even if your fitness goals change, this book will still be useful. An added advantage is that you don't need any bulky fitness equipment, so it won't take over the spare room and you won't have to break the household budget.

All the exercises in this book have been tried and tested by experts in the field and found to be very effective. They really do work, so let's get started!

The 6-minute concept

How easy would it be for you to devote 6 minutes in the morning to exercise? Even if you usually jump out of bed and dash straight off to work without time for breakfast, it's really not much of a sacrifice to make, especially when you consider the results you can achieve.

Six minutes is the average time it takes you to brush your teeth and have a wash, or to make a cup of coffee and eat a bowl of cereal. What we're trying to say is that, even if you're usually pushed for time in the morning, it won't be hard to negotiate a spare 6 minutes into your timetable. Even if you have to set your alarm clock a full 6 minutes earlier than usual, it's very unlikely to affect your quality of sleep or leave you tired during the day, so you won't feel hard done by. In fact, making time for exercise in the morning will give you a fantastic energy boost that should last all day. That's on top of a great new physique, which will really give you something to brag about.

Exercise is also known to boost levels of 'happy hormones' (endorphins) in the brain, making you feel more cheerful and relaxed, with a higher sense of self-esteem. Endorphins also beat stress, so you'll not only be a dream to work with, but you're also more likely to perform to your best abilities. And, when you're feeling optimistic, you're more likely to make healthy food choices, which will further help you to achieve your goals. Plus, since you'll get your workout done in the morning, it doesn't matter if you have to work late or fulfil social commitments in the evening – which you might be tempted to use as an excuse not to do your exercise routine.

An added bonus of exercising in the morning is that, since it's done on an empty stomach, you're more likely to burn fat reserves rather then simply work off food that's sitting in your stomach. It will also kickstart your metabolism, helping you burn more calories throughout the day – although that's not an excuse to eat an extra doughnut!

INTRODUCTION

If you're naturally cynical, you might be wondering whether 6 minutes of exercise is enough to make a difference to your body. The good news is that it works. It's true that some fitness fanatics swear by hours of cardio for weight loss and fat burning, but studies have shown that spending a short time exercising at a high intensity (i.e. doing something that gets your heart rate pumping and makes you slightly out of breath) can be more effective than exercising at a moderate level for longer periods of time.

It's the good news we've all been waiting for and it's why we've created this handy book, so anyone with an interest in fitness can make a real difference to their body without it costing a fortune or having to spend hours working out in the gym. Now, all you have to decide is what you want to focus on each morning.

Four ways to fitness

This book is divided into four sections, each of which targets a common trouble zone or offers a total body workout. Each section is thoroughly explained later in the book, but if you don't yet know what you want to focus on, here is an insight into what each section can help you achieve.

Stretching

Targets: All the major muscles in the body – to make them longer, leaner and more toned.
What's involved: A series of challenging stretches that will leave your mind calm and your body more flexible.
Who it will suit: If you're stressed you'll benefit from this relaxing routine, but it's also great if you want to prevent your muscles from becoming bulky.

Body toning

Targets: Each of the major muscle groups in the body – it's an all-over workout.

What's involved: A wide variety of exercises that are fun to do, including squats, lunges, sidekicks, stepping, crunches, press-ups and lifting dumbbells.

Who it will suit: People who want to see an all-over improvement in muscle tone and shape and who want to target the whole body instead of specific trouble zones.

Flat stomach

Targets: The four abdominal muscle groups that support your lower back, protect the internal organs, maintain your posture and allow you to bend, twist and sit up. They all look fabulous when trim and toned!

What's involved: Seated exercises such as knee lifts, and ones that you can do on the floor like pelvic tilts, plus a series of curls (mini sit-ups).

Who it will suit: Apple-shaped women (who tend to store fat around the middle) and new mums wanting to tone up saggy skin.

Hips and thighs

Targets: Like it says on the box, this section targets your hips, thighs and those stubborn pockets of fat around the tops of the legs that are so hard to shift.

What's involved: A series of squats, lunges, seated and standing exercises, plus a lot that you can do lying on the floor.

Who it will suit: Anyone who struggles to shift fat from their lower half.

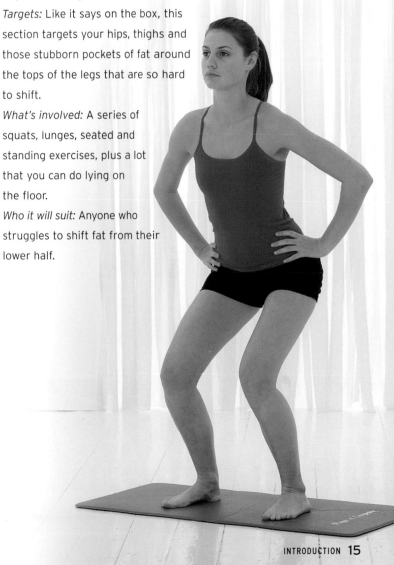

Warming up, cooling down

As with all forms of exercise, it's vitally important that you spend time warming up before you start and cooling down before you finish. Not only will it help prepare your muscles for exercise by making them more receptive, but it will also protect you from stiffness and injuries such as strains and cramp.

If you turn to pages 24–35, you'll find 16 easy exercises – 11 warm-ups and 5 cool-downs – from which you can pick and choose in order to ease yourself in and out of the 6-minute plan. If you choose to do the hips and thighs, flat stomach or body toning plan, you should spend around 1 minute warming up and the same time cooling down. Make sure you carry out each warm-up exercise for no less than 20 seconds and each cool-down exercise for 10 seconds. Your body will thank you for it.

If you're doing the stretching plan, warming up and cooling down isn't necessary because the exercises in this section aren't strenuous enough to cause damage to the muscles. Instead, prior to the stretching plan, make sure you've had a brisk walk around your bedroom or a quick jog on the spot, because this will get the circulation going.

If you do feel any discomfort while carrying out any of the exercises, it's important that you stop what you're doing immediately and take a break. If you ever experience a nagging pain, or feel sick, dizzy or unusually out of breath at any time while doing the exercises, simply stop and book an appointment with your doctor to rule out any underlying health problems that might be causing the discomfort. It might put your workout plan on hold for a while, but it's best to be safe when it comes to your health.

If your muscles feel sore at any time (if you're not used to exercise, you're most likely to experience this during the first few days of doing the plan), then take some time out to rest until your muscles feel good enough to get going again. As long as you pick up from where you left off and finish the two-week plan without any major disruptions, the effects will be the same.

If you're a complete beginner, you may want to ease yourself gently into the plan and do less repetition. That's fine if you do, just remember to be persistent and your efforts will pay off. Soon enough, you'll find that your body will be better able to cope with the routine and, when this happens, you'll know you've made amazing progress. Just stay positive, enthusiastic and optimistic and you'll reap the rewards.

What to wear

Wearing the right kit can make a massive difference to your performance. What's vitally important is that you don't just roll out of bed and get started while you're still in your pyjamas. Not only might this restrict your movement, but you could trip over baggy clothes, for example, and you won't be in the right frame of mind for exercise.

A breathable Lycra sports top or a fitted T-shirt coupled with stretchy leggings or shorts is the ideal combination. You can pick up some great gear in the sports shop but, if you're on a budget, an old pair of tracksuit bottoms and a fitted vest top should be just fine. The good news is that exercising at home means that you won't get spotted by friends or colleagues in less-than-flattering attire.

If you're exercising on carpet or in the garage, you can do so in trainers. Alternatively, if you're working out on a wooden floor or lino, make sure you stay barefoot to save you from slipping.

If you have long hair, tie back loose ends with a clip or Alice band to stop it hanging in front of your eyes - that way you'll be able to read this book and follow the plan without a problem.

What you'll need

Equipment: The great thing about this workout plan is that you don't need any expensive equipment. However, you could invest in a padded exercise mat to stop you from slipping, a stopwatch so you can accurately time the exercises, and some dumbbells that you feel comfortable using (ask a shop assistant to help you choose a suitable starting weight). If you don't have the cash, a tin of beans makes a good dumbbell because it's easy to hold.

Space: Make sure you clear a space that is big enough for you to move freely in – that means one where you can fully extend your arms and legs without hitting anything. This may involve a bit of furniture reshuffling, but clearing a space especially for exercise and using it every day means you're more likely to stick to the plan as you get used to the routine.

How to use this book

If you're keen to make a start on getting a fabulous new body, it may be tempting to try to combine a few of the sections at once. However, we recommend that you stick to one section at a time and finish each two-week plan before moving on to another section. This way, your attention will be focused on carrying out the exercises to the best of your ability, and you won't find yourself cutting corners or trying to achieve more than is necessary.

We recommend that, before you begin, you have a thorough read of the section you want to complete. This will help you familiarize yourself with the different exercises so you won't waste time wondering exactly how to do them when you start. Remember to spend time warming up, then move straight on to the 6-minute exercise plan and, once you've finished, on to the cool-down exercises.

The two-week guide at the end of each section lists six exercises (with page references) that you should hold, or repeat (as directed), usually for 30 seconds. Once you've finished all six, simply repeat the routine to make it last for the full 6

minutes. It's as easy as that. The two-week plans are a rough guide, so if you find any particular exercises tricky, feel free to replace them with something else. However, the closer you stick to the plan we've drawn up, the better you'll find the results will be.

We encourage you to stick to your chosen section (hips and thighs, flat stomach, body toning or stretching) for two weeks, because this is the perfect amount of time you will need in order to see results. If you make sure that you include occasional rest days, it's fine to run the plans one after another. The more you do, the better you'll look and feel.

Getting started

As with all exercise programmes, it's important that you discuss this workout plan with your doctor before you start. This is important in order to rule out any health conditions that may prevent you from taking part. Hopefully, you'll be given the green light and a pat on the back, and then there'll be no stopping you!

Posture: Having good posture makes all the exercises easier to do and more effective, too. Good posture results from your spine maintaining its natural curve, without sagging. If your posture is incorrect, every movement you make will be inefficient, leading to weakness, aching joints and muscles, and an increased risk of injury.

Test your posture by standing on one leg - you should be able to balance without wobbling. Even if you do wobble, the good news is that certain exercises in this book, such as those in the body toning and hips and thighs sections, will naturally improve your posture because they strengthen the major muscles (the core muscles) that support your body.

The basic thing to remember is, if you're standing, imagine your spine is extended beyond your head up towards the sky and that someone is pulling on the end to make you stand to attention, a bit like a puppet on a string. Make sure your shoulders are relaxed – an easy way to check is to roll them backwards a few times. This will help you find their natural resting place.

Another point to watch out for is that your stomach muscles are 'engaged' at all times, which basically means that they are pulled in, nice and tight. This will automatically prevent your back from curving, making the exercises more effective and guarding you against injury. Make sure you bear all this in mind at all times when exercising.

Keeping elbows and knees soft: If an exercise requires you to extend your arms or legs, remember always to keep elbows and knees 'soft' (slightly bent). It will prevent you getting injured.

Breathing: The correct way to breathe when exercising is to breathe in slowly through your nose (notice how your abdominal cavity rises as you do so), and breathe out slowly through your mouth. Make sure you continue to breathe in and out regularly throughout. And don't hold your breath – this will cause your blood pressure to rise, which can be dangerous.

Lastly, keep a bottle of water close by – keeping hydrated means the muscles work better and you'll be less likely to get cramp. Now, you're set to go. Simply pick one of the four sections and begin!

Warming up is **essential** before you begin any kind of strenuous physical **exercise**, to **protect** your muscles from strain. Likewise, **cooling down** helps the muscles **relax** and wind down after exercise.

warm up/
cool down

Tempting though it is to save time by launching yourself straight into an exercise routine, if you don't warm up you are highly likely to injure yourself because cold muscles and joints are less flexible and more prone to strain. So the 6-minute routines do assume that you will have done your warming up beforehand.

Waist twist

It's important not to move your hips and knees during this exercise, but do feel free to move your arms like a hula dancer if it helps you get into the right mood!

1 Stand up straight with your knees slightly bent (soft, rather than 'locked'). Keep your feet hip-width apart and your hands resting on your hips.

2 Tighten your abdominal muscles by pulling your navel back towards your spine.

3 Keeping your hips and knees still, rotate your shoulders and head to the right, then return to the centre.

4 Now twist to the left, rotating your head and shoulders and keeping your hips and knees still.

5 Repeat this exercise a further five times on each side.

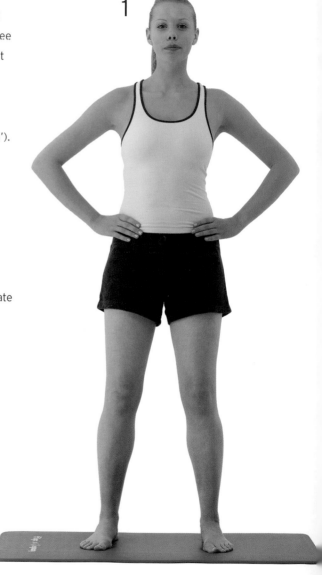

1

3

Hip circles

This exercise will mobilize your lower abdominal muscles. Try to make sure that only your pelvis is rocking rather than your torso.

1 Stand up straight with your knees slightly bent, feet hip-width apart, hands resting on your hips.

2 Tighten your abdominal muscles by gently pulling your navel towards your spine. This movement should feel light and subtle – do not suck in your waist or hold your breath.

3 Gently rotate your pelvis to the right so that you are rotating in a full circle.

4 Repeat nine times to the right then circle ten times to the left.

WARM UP

Forward bend

With this exercise, bend only as far as is comfortable – you don't have to touch your toes. Remember, you'll be able to stretch farther as time goes by and you become more supple with exercise.

1 Stand up straight with your feet hip-width apart and your knees slightly bent rather than locked. Place your hands, palms downwards, on the front of your thighs.

2 Tighten your abdominal muscles by gently pulling in your navel toward your backbone.

3 Slowly slide your hands down your legs towards your toes. Try not to overarch your back.

Flatter stomach in a flash

A very simple way of making your stomach look flatter is simply to make sure your posture is correct. Good posture happens when your spine is in natural alignment rather than hunched or slouched. For an instant, more streamlined appearance, stand with your feet hip-width apart. Gently pull up through your legs, keeping your knees slightly bent. Lengthen your spine, pull in your stomach muscles, and stand tall. Keep your shoulders down and relaxed so that your neck is as long as possible. Voilà – as if by magic, your stomach will look flatter!

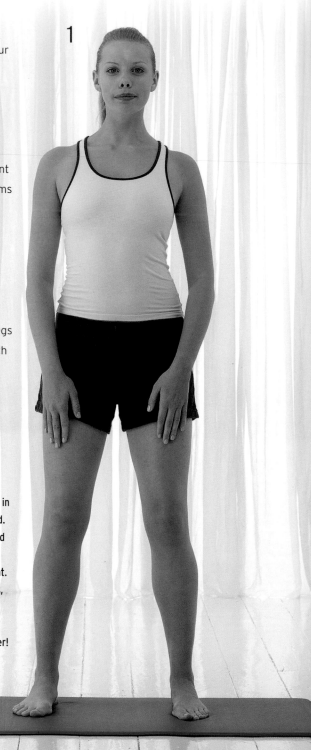

1

4 Position yourself so you feel a stretch in the hamstrings at the back of your legs but don't stretch so far that it hurts.

5 Hold for a count of three then return to the centre (see step 1).

6 Repeat four more times. Keep your breathing steady throughout.

WATCH POINT
Never stretch to the point of pain.

3

Side bends

Do not do this exercise quickly with your arms above your head because this will make it hard to control the movement.

1 Stand up straight with your feet hip-width apart, your knees slightly bent, and your arms by your sides.

2 Tighten your abdominal muscles by gently pulling your navel towards your spine.

3 Keeping your back straight and without leaning forwards, slowly bend to one side from the waist so that your hand slides down the side of your leg. Straighten up again.

4 Repeat on the other side. Repeat four more times on each side.

3

Knee bends

This exercise loosens the hip flexor muscles and helps warm up all the leg muscles. Don't lock your knees as you do this, and bend only as far as is comfortable.

1 Stand with one hand resting on a support such as a high-backed chair or a table, your feet hip-width apart and slightly turned out. Tighten your abdominal muscles.

2 Slowly bend your knees and lower your hips, then straighten up again. Use your buttock and leg muscles to lower and straighten.

3 Repeat nine times.

WATCH POINT
Never point your toes inwards while exercising – this can damage your knees.

2

Marching

This warming-up exercise will help to raise your body temperature and increase blood flow to the muscles. March on the spot for at least a minute, swinging your arms and gradually raising your knees higher as you go (but not so that you're goose-stepping). Make sure your breathing is deep and regular as you march. Once you feel warm, take the time to perform a few stretching exercises.

Leg swings

This exercise warms up the hip joints. Don't swing your legs too high (about 45 degrees is high enough), and keep the movements controlled and flowing.

1 Stand with one hand resting on a support, such as a high-backed chair or a table, and balance on one leg with the knee slightly bent. Tighten your abdominal muscles to protect your back.

2 Gently swing your other leg forwards and backwards. Keep your hips still as your leg moves from back to front. Swing up to 20 times on one leg then swap sides and swing on the other leg.

2

Standing knee lift

This exercise mobilizes the quadriceps and the hip flexors at the front of your body.

1 Stand up straight with your left hand on a chair to balance you.

2 Tighten your abdominal muscles.

3 Pull up your right knee so that your foot is parallel to your left knee.

4 Release and repeat on the other leg.

5 Repeat nine more times on each leg.

Standing leg circles

This exercise warms up the buttock muscles by lifting and drawing them together.

1 Stand up straight with good posture with your knees soft and legs hip-width apart. For balance hold on to a chair.

2 Tighten your abdominal muscles by gently pulling in your navel towards your backbone.

3 Lift your left leg 5 cm (2 inches) off the floor and gently circle it one way, then the other.

4 Return to the starting position and repeat on the other leg.

5 Repeat nine more times on each leg.

Standing quad stretch

1 Stand up straight with your feet hip-width apart and your knees soft (slightly bent). Tighten your stomach muscles to protect your back.

2 Bend one leg up behind you and hold your foot or ankle with your hand.

3 Hold for 5-10 seconds then release and repeat on the other side.

4 Repeat twice more on each leg.

Standing hamstring stretch

1 Stand up straight with your knees hip-width apart and your knees soft (slightly bent).

2 Extend one foot forwards so that it is pointing in front of you with the weight resting on its heel. Tighten your abdominal muscles to protect your back.

3 Rest your hands on the thigh of the bent leg to support your body weight.

4 Bend forwards from the hip and feel the stretch in the back of the thigh of the straight leg.

5 Hold for 5-10 seconds then release and repeat on the other side.

6 Repeat twice more on each leg.

2

4

Train your brain

Use your mind to help you get the most from your workout. Focus on what you are doing correctly. As you are exercising, tell yourself how well you are doing. Think of each muscle contracting and stretching as you do your routine. This can make you do even better, whereas concentrating on what you are doing wrong sets you up to fail. You can even use visualizations to convince yourself that your body is becoming fitter and more toned!

COOL DOWN

Cooling down after exercise is just as important as warming up. As well as helping to prevent dizziness and a sudden drop in body temperature (which can make you feel unwell), cooling down realigns working muscles to their normal position to avoid post-exercise tightness and stiffness. It also helps you to relax and gives you a few quiet moments to yourself before carrying on with the rest of your day. Cooling-down stretches can be held for longer than 10 seconds because the muscles are warm.

Leg lift and cross

1 Lie on your back with your legs out straight and your arms stretched out to the sides.

2 Breathe in to prepare, and tighten your abdominal muscles. Lift your right leg up to the ceiling as you breathe out, and flex your foot.

3 Using your abdominal muscles to control the movement, lower your leg across your body over to the left side until the foot touches the floor.

4 Hold for a count of 20 then slowly return to the starting position. Repeat on the other side.

WATCH POINT
If you can't take your foot all the way to the floor, bend your arm up to meet your foot and rest the foot on your hand.

Lying full body stretch

1 Lie flat on your back and relax. Breathe in and extend your arms outwards and backwards so that they meet behind your head. Try to keep your arms on the floor throughout the movement but if this isn't possible just keep them as low as you can.

2 Gently stretch out your body from your fingertips to your toes. Your lower back may lift from the floor a little.

3 Hold for a count of 20 then slowly release, bring your arms back down to your sides, and relax.

WATCH POINT

If you have any back problems, keep your knees bent slightly throughout. Also be aware that, if you are unused to stretching, you may feel tightness in your shoulders or cramp in your feet – in which case, relax. You will be able to hold this stretch for longer with practice.

1

2

COOL DOWN

Hip and thigh stretch

1 Kneel with one knee above the ankle and foot flat on the floor, and stretch your other leg behind you so that the knee touches the floor.

2 Place your hands on your front knee to balance yourself. Hold this position for a count of ten then repeat on the other leg.

WATCH POINT
Be sure to pull in your abdominal muscles during the whole of the hip and thigh stretch in order to protect your back.

2

Standing full body stretch

1 Stand tall with your arms by your sides and your feet hip-width apart.

2 Raise your arms above your head and clasp your hands together.

3 Stretch your arms up as high as possible and feel the stretch in your arms, chest, stomach, hips and thighs. Hold for a count of ten, then release.

Knee hug

1 Lie on your back with your legs straight. Tighten your abdominal muscles and pull both legs up to your chest.

2 Take hold of your knees and hug your knees tighter to your chest. Hold for a count of ten.

3 Release the pull then repeat as many times as you wish.

Stretching is an excellent way to keep your body in shape. Not only is it soothing, it will help your muscles to stay flexible and protect them from injury. It will also help you look longer and leaner.

stretching

INTRODUCTION

Stretching every day not only counters the muscle-shortening effects of exercise, it can work wonders for your mind, too. Many fitness trainers recommend their clients take up stretching once they've hit a plateau with exercise because it develops the muscles in a different way to cardio or other weight-based exercise.

The best thing about stretching is that it'll make you look longer and leaner. Plus, this section will prove that you don't have to jump up and down in order to streamline your silhouette.

This section is perfect if you have an existing medical condition such as asthma, and you are unable to do more strenuous forms of exercise. However, some of the stretches will make you slightly out of breath, so concentrate on keeping your breathing steady.

The benefits

Soothing music is ideal to accompany stretching exercises, and this routine will help calm your mind for the day to follow – it's almost like meditating. Physically, stretching will help tone and lengthen your muscles and it will also make you more flexible. Doing it regularly will help reduce the risk of injury to the joints, muscles and tendons while exercising and it's a great way of relieving any soreness or tension you feel after a gruelling workout.

Stretching is also a great way to stimulate the lymphatic system, which in turn helps to cleanse the body of toxins and boost circulation. So, it's a great way to kickstart a detox and help keep cellulite at bay.

Effective stretching

The 34 stretches in this section aim to stretch out each of the major muscle groups – the thighs, bottom, calves, ankles, stomach, waist, arms, shoulders, chest, back and neck. Each stretch lasts for around 30 seconds and you should aim to hold each stretch for three sets of 10 seconds, with a brief pause in between. In order to make the routine effective, it's important that you don't stop for more than a minute between exercises. Like all exercise, stretching has cumulative effects, so keep going!

What you'll need

For this routine you'll need a non-slip mat and a chair, and for some exercises you'll need to be near a wall for support. You don't need to spend one minute warming

WATCH POINT
It can be tempting to 'bounce'
while in a stretch – for example, if you're trying
to push yourself while reaching for the floor.
However, this can strain the muscles
so avoid it at all costs.

up or cooling down to do this workout, but take a brisk walk around your room or jump up and down on the spot for a few seconds to make sure you're warm.

Once you've got used to the routine, if you feel you can increase certain stretches, do so slowly and gently by moving further into position. Just remember to take your time and not to push yourself. You'll be amazed at how far you can go when you put the practice in and you'll be lithe and limber in no time at all.

Note: If you ever develop a persistent pain by doing any of the stretches in this routine, see your doctor for advice.

THIGHS

Seated hamstring stretch

The hamstrings are the muscles running up the backs of the thighs to your bottom. It's common for people to suffer with tight hamstrings, especially if they do a lot of sport, which is why it's great to stretch them out. If you don't stretch, tight hamstrings can cause the hips and pelvis to rotate backwards, resulting in bad posture.

1 Sit down on the floor with your legs straight out in front of you, keeping your feet flexed. Sit up straight so your back isn't hunched and place your hands on your hips.

2 Lean forwards from the hips, letting your upper body drop down towards your feet. You can extend your arms and try to touch your toes, although if you do this, make sure that you don't curve your back.

3 Hold for 10 seconds but don't bounce. Return to the starting position and repeat twice more.

WATCH POINT
This stretch works both hamstrings at the same time so you get double the benefit!

1

2

Inner thigh stretch

This stretch targets the muscles in the inner thighs, which are called the adductors. It's an easy way to stretch both the legs at once and is great if you combine it with a short meditation.

1 Sit on the floor with knees bent and soles of your feet pressed together so you're in a 'frog' position. Hold the soles of your feet together with both hands.

2 Sit up, so your back is straight, and pull your stomach muscles in towards your spine.

3 Using the muscles in your inner thighs, push your knees down towards the floor. Make sure you don't bounce your knees.

4 When you've got your knees as far as you can go, hold the stretch for 10 seconds. Slowly release, then hold for two more sets of 10 seconds.

WATCH POINT

Make sure you don't curl your back. It makes it easier to reach the floor, but you'll be making the stretch less effective.

THIGHS

Hip flexor stretch

This stretch targets the hip flexors (the iliopsoas muscles) as well as the muscles at the front of the thighs. It may feel like a small movement but it has great results. It works really well at easing away the tension in the muscles that may have built up if you've been sitting down for most of the day.

1 Stand with feet hip-width apart and hands resting on your waist.

2 Extend your right leg directly out behind you by about 30 cm (12 inches). Keep both feet flat on the floor.

3 Bend both knees so your whole body drops down towards the floor by 5 cm (2 inches).

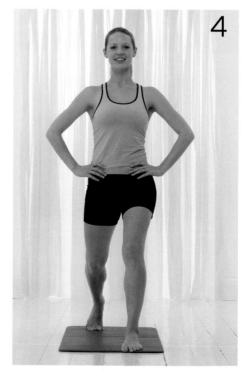

4 Letting your heel naturally lift off the floor, tilt your pelvis forwards, bringing your bottom forwards and your hips up. You should immediately feel the stretch in the hip and down the front of the thigh of the extended leg.

5 Hold the stretch for around 7 seconds, gently release then hold for another 7 seconds. Repeat with the left leg.

WATCH POINT
You can stay close to a wall or a chair in case you need support.

Don't allow your knees to drift apart while you're
holding the stretch, or you won't be targeting the
quads effectively.

2

Quadriceps stretch

The quadriceps muscles are found at the front of your thighs and are often referred to as the 'quads'. Depending on how flexible you are, this stretch may feel quite hard to do at first but it quickly becomes easier. If, on the other hand, you need to feel a bigger stretch, simply thrust slightly forwards the hip of the leg you are stretching.

1 Stand at a right angle to the back of a chair and hold the back with your left hand for support.

2 Keeping your knees together, bend your right leg backwards, grab your right foot or ankle with your right hand, and bring your heel towards your bottom. Make sure you keep your left leg straight, with the knee soft (not locked) and your left foot flat on the floor.

3 Hold the stretch for around 7 seconds, slowly release, then hold for another 7 seconds. Repeat with the left leg.

THIGHS

Touch the floor

This stretch targets all the tendons and muscles at the backs of your legs, including the hamstrings and the calves. You should start practising this stretch with legs quite wide apart and, as you get more supple, bring them closer together.

1 Stand with feet slightly more than hip-width apart and arms resting by your sides.

2 Slowly bend over from the waist and reach down to touch the floor. If you can't reach the floor just go as far as you can.

3 Hold the stretch for three sets of 10 seconds, returning to the start position in-between. Do not bounce.

WATCH POINT
Remember to let your head and neck relax – it's tempting to look out in front of you but this will only increase your chances of pulling a muscle in your neck.

Deep lunge

Holding your body in a deep lunge position will really help to stretch out the quads in the extended leg. The deep lunge is commonly used as part of yoga routines, and if you continue to breathe deeply throughout the stretch, you'll find it really relaxing too.

1 Stand with feet 15 cm (6 inches) apart with your hands resting on your hips.

2 Lunge forwards with your right leg so your right knee is bent and your leg is at a right angle to the floor. Make sure your knee doesn't travel beyond your toe. Your right foot should be flat on the floor.

3 Lean forwards and place your hands either side of your right foot. Your left leg should be stretched out behind you with the ball of your foot balancing on the floor.

4 Hold for two sets of 7 seconds on your right leg, returning to the start position in-between, and then repeat with the left leg.

WATCH POINT
Keep your extended leg straight at all times so your knee doesn't touch the floor. This will help make the stretch as beneficial as possible.

2

3

BOTTOM

Piriformis stretch

The piriformis muscles lie deep in the gluteal muscles (the ones in your bottom). This is a good stretch to rejuvenate your backside after a long night's sleep.

1 Lie on the floor on your back with both your knees bent, your feet flat on the floor, and palms down by your sides.

2 Lift your right leg off the ground and, rotating your leg from the hip, cross it over so the ankle of your right foot rests just above your left knee. Your right knee should be pointing to the right.

3 Grasp your left thigh with both hands and gently pull your left leg off the floor towards your chest. You will feel the stretch in the outside of your right leg.

4 Hold for two sets of 7 seconds on your right leg and then repeat with the left leg.

WATCH POINT
Make sure you are relaxed all the way through the exercise so that you don't end up locking your hip, and your shoulders remain tension-free.

2

3

Seated gluteal stretch

This is a great way to stretch out the muscles in your bottom, while sitting on it! It's quite a hard move to perfect, but the deep, intense stretch will give great results.

1 Sit on the floor with your back straight to create a good posture.

2 Extend your right leg straight out in front of you, keeping your foot flexed.

3 Bend the knee of your left leg and bring it towards you so your left foot is flat on the floor.

4 Cross your left foot over your right leg, so your left foot is level with your right knee.

5 Take your right arm and hug your left knee. Pull it towards your right shoulder until you feel the stretch. Your body should be twisted from the waist. Look to the left.

6 Hold for two sets of 7 seconds, and then repeat with the other leg.

WATCH POINT
If you want to get the best stretch you can, don't lean back. Keep your back straight and the stretch will be more effective.

Cross and dip

This stretch targets the same muscles as the Seated gluteal stretch, but it will also develop your balance. The stretch will get easier as your calves become more flexible, because you'll be able to lower yourself down further without letting your foot rise up off the floor.

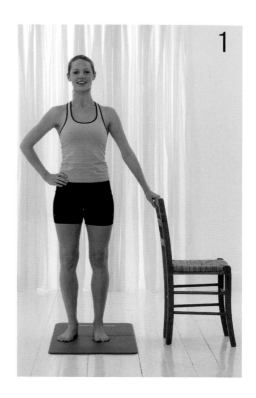

1 Stand behind a chair at a right-angle to it with feet hip-width apart and knees soft. Hold on to the back of the chair with your left hand for support.

2 Bend your right leg and bring your right foot across to meet your left leg, so it's resting above your left knee.

3 Slowly bend the knee of your left leg and lower yourself down towards the floor. Your left foot should remain flat on the floor at all times.

4 As you go down, your left knee should push your right foot higher into the air, which is when you should start to feel the stretch in your right hip, buttock and top of thigh.

5 Once you've gone down as far as you can, hold the stretch for two sets of 7 seconds. Repeat with the other leg.

WATCH POINT
Keep your back straight at all times; it will stop you from getting a bad back.

Bend and stretch

This is a tried and tested stretch that targets all the muscles at the back of the thighs and in the bottom. Look forwards towards the toes of your extended leg while you are doing the stretch, because it will inspire you to go as far as you can.

1 Stand a large step away from the front of a chair, with feet hip-width apart.

2 Lift your right leg and rest your right foot firmly on the seat of the chair. Your hands should be on your hips.

3 Bend over from the waist, and reach out to touch the toes of your right foot with both hands. You should feel the stretch in your right buttock and thigh.

4 Hold for two sets of 7 seconds on your right leg, without bouncing, and then repeat with the left leg.

WATCH POINT
Make sure that the chair is in the right position – you don't want the foot of your extended leg to be dangling off the edge.

2

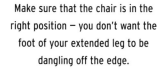

3

Runner's calf stretch

As the name suggests, if you do a lot of running or walking you may find that your calves feel tight and inflexible. This stretch will help them feel loose and tension-free.

1 Get down on the floor on your hands and knees, with your knees resting directly below your hips and your hands below your shoulders. Curl your toes under so they are resting on the floor.

2 Push up off the floor with both hands and straighten your legs, pushing your bottom into the air. Your elbows and knees should be soft.

1

3 Try to lower your heels gently to the floor. Hold for three sets of 10 seconds, returning to the start position in-between.

WATCH POINT
This is quite a difficult stretch and you may not be able to hold it for the full 10 seconds at first. Just try your best and don't give up.

2

Push-off calf stretch

You usually see joggers doing this stretch before a big run – that's because it's a really good way of performing a controlled calf stretch that targets the gastrocnemius muscle (the big muscle at the back of the calf). To get the best stretch possible, make sure your full weight is shifted towards the wall.

1 Stand at arm's length from the wall, with your feet shoulder-width apart.

2 Extend your right leg out in front of you and bend your right knee.

3 Place the palms of your hands, at shoulder height, flat against the wall.

4 Take one step back with your left leg and, keeping it straight, press your heel firmly into the floor. You should feel the stretch in the calf of your left leg. Keep your hips facing the wall and your rear leg and spine in a straight line.

5 Hold the stretch for two sets of 7 seconds, then repeat with the other leg.

WATCH POINT
If you want to feel a greater stretch, simply move your extended leg a little bit further away from the wall.

4

2

CALVES & ANKLES

Soleus stretch

The soleus muscle is a small muscle in the calf, which is situated slightly lower down in the leg, under the gastrocnemius. It's usually quite hard to target, but this stretch will give it a good once-over.

1 Stand in front of a wall with feet shoulder-width apart and flat on the floor.

2 Bend your knees and drop your buttocks down towards the floor a short way.

3 Place your palms flat against the wall and gently lean towards the wall until you feel the stretch in your lower calf muscles. Hold for three sets of 10 seconds.

WATCH POINT

This is a more subtle stretch than those that target the gastrocnemius muscles. If you're finding it hard to feel the stretch, simply step back a bit from the wall and bend your knees a little bit more.

3

Point and flex stretch

This is a really easy stretch to do and it may remind you of having dance classes as a child. It's best to keep doing the movement explained below rather than holding the stretch for a set period of time. Make sure you put the effort into really pointing and flexing the feet – the further you go, the better the stretch.

1 Sit on the floor with both legs stretched out in front of you. Sit upright with your back straight and your hands resting on the floor by your bottom for support.

2 Start by flexing your feet towards you as far as you can get them. Then, point them away from you down to the floor as far as you can.

3 Keep repeating the movement slowly until the 30 seconds are up.

WATCH POINT
Try not to rush the movement. Your priority is to feel the stretch rather than do as many repetitions as you can in the time allowed.

2

STOMACH & WAIST

Push down

The Push down is a great warm-up for the stomach and waist. It's a really gentle movement that helps to get you warm, while stretching out your major muscles.

1 Stand with feet hip-width apart and your hands resting by your sides. Make sure your legs are straight with knees soft.

2 Lean to the right, sliding your right arm down your right thigh towards your knee as you go. Keep your back straight and your head and neck in line with your spine at all times. You should feel the stretch in your left side.

3 Hold for two sets of seven seconds, returning to the starting position in-between, then repeat on your left side.

WATCH POINT
You don't need to tilt over very far, just aim to touch the side of your knee with your hand.

2

Up and over

This exercise is an old-style way of targeting the muscles at the side of your waist, which are called the obliques. It's a great way of stretching out your love handles and it also helps you to feel really refreshed in the morning.

1 Stand with feet hip-width apart and your hands resting by your sides. Make sure your legs are slightly bent with knees soft. Keep your back straight and your head and neck in line with your spine.

2 Raise your left arm over your head and lean over from the waist to the right, so that your right hand travels down the side of your right leg. Your left arm should be reaching up and over your head. You should feel the stretch in the left side of your waist.

3 Hold for two sets of 7 seconds then slowly return to the starting position and repeat on the other side.

WATCH POINT
Don't try to stretch down too far –
just do enough to feel it working.

Twist

The Twist is another great way of stretching out your obliques. This movement will help you develop long and lean muscles to support a trim waist. You're only supposed to feel a subtle stretch, so don't make the mistake of twisting round too far in order to feel a greater one.

1 Stand with feet hip-width apart. Your feet should be flat on the floor and toes should be facing forwards.

2 Extend both arms out to the sides, at shoulder height.

3 Keeping your arms straight, gently rotate from the hip round to the left. Your hips and pelvis should remain facing forwards.

4 Hold the position for two sets of 7 seconds, until you feel the stretch in your waist. Slowly return to the starting position then repeat on your right side.

3

WATCH POINT
Knees should always
be soft to help mobilize
your upper body. As
with all stretches,
don't bounce.

Full body stretch

You need to find a large space on the floor to do this stretch where nothing will get in the way of you fully extending your arms and legs. This stretch will target the abdominals – the muscles across your stomach.

1 Lie on the floor on your back with your legs straight. Take your arms back above your head so they are also stretched out as far as possible.

2 Make sure the small of your back is pressed into the floor and pull in your stomach muscles towards your spine.

3 Extend your fingertips and toes as far as you can. You should feel the stretch across your stomach.

4 Hold for three sets of 10 seconds, gently pausing to release in-between.

WATCH POINT
This is also good for giving your body an all-over general stretch, so it's a good one to choose to start or end your routine. It makes a particularly relaxing cool-down exercise for the other exercise plans.

4

Oblique stretch

This is an easy way to give the muscles in your waist a really good stretch. As you walk your hands around to get into position, you may not be able to reach your knees but that's fine – just go as far round as you can comfortably.

1 Get down on the floor on all fours with your knees resting directly below your hips and your hands below your shoulders.

2 Keeping your knees where they are, walk both your hands around to your right-hand side to meet your knees, so you are twisting from the waist. You should feel the stretch down your left-hand side. Hold the stretch for 10 seconds then walk the hands back round to the starting position.

3 Repeat the movement so you are stretching round to the left-hand side.

WATCH POINT
Pull your stomach muscles in while you do this exercise – it will help to stop your back from arching.

STOMACH & WAIST

Hip mobilization

You'll feel this stretch across your stomach, as you circle your hips around. It's also a great way of loosening up your hips, so it's a good stretch for starting the day.

1 Stand with feet slightly further than hip-width apart.

2 Rest your hands on your waist and begin by slowly rotating your hips clockwise in a circular motion. Make sure you are in control of the movement and your legs stay slightly bent with feet firmly on the ground. To get the movement right, keep your back straight and try not to stick your bottom out.

3 After 15 seconds, repeat the same movement but this time in an anticlockwise direction.

WATCH POINT

You should be rotating from the hips, which, when done correctly, shouldn't cause your back to arch or give you any pain. Practise this one before you start the routine – you'll be able to tell when you're doing it right by the way it feels.

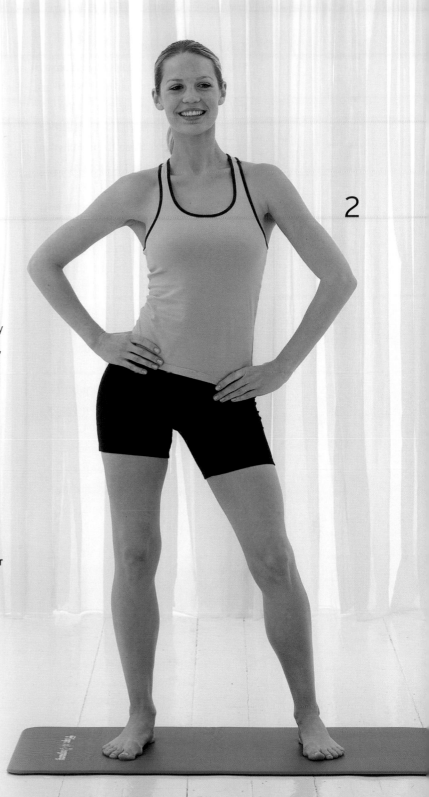

2

Shoulder stretch

This is an easy stretch to do, and will really get your shoulders loosened up. It's great to do if you've been particularly stressed-out recently, because it will help to get rid of any built-up tension.

1 You can do this stretch from either a standing or a seated position. Extend your right arm directly out in front of you so it's parallel with the floor.

2 Using your left hand, grip the back of your right arm between your elbow and your shoulder and use it to bring your right arm gently across the front of your chest. You should feel the stretch down the inner side of your right arm and across your right shoulder blade.

3 Hold the position for two sets of 7 seconds and then repeat with the other arm.

WATCH POINT
Stop yourself from rotating by making sure your hips are facing forwards at all times.

Pec stretch

Your pectoral muscles (pecs) are the big muscles that sit under your bust. Stretching them out will help get rid of any knots or tension that may have built up from carrying heavy bags. Plus, this stretch will help encourage deep breathing, which will enable you to feel a whole lot perkier and more refreshed in the morning.

1 Stand with feet hip-width apart. Place your palms on your lower back then gently pull your shoulders back together and stick your chest out until you feel the stretch. Keep your elbows soft.

2 Hold the stretch for three sets of 10 seconds.

WATCH POINT
When you bring your shoulders back, be careful not to arch your back. All the movement should come from the shoulders.

1

Inner arm stretch

This targets all the muscles in your upper arms – you'll be surprised at how easy it is to feel the stretch.

1 Stand in an open door frame, with your abs tight and body straight.

2 Hold on to the door frame with your left hand just below shoulder level, or as high as is comfortable. Take a big step forwards so your left arm is extended out behind you. Keeping your hips facing forwards and your head and neck in line with your spine, rotate your upper body to the right until you feel the stretch in your left arm. Lean forwards to feel a greater stretch.

3 Hold for two sets of 7 seconds then turn around, step forwards and repeat the stretch with your right arm.

WATCH POINT
Don't worry if you find it difficult to get your arm up to shoulder height because you can still achieve a good stretch by having it slightly lower.

Bicep stretch

The bicep muscles are the big muscles at the front of your upper arms. It's good to stretch them out so you develop long, lean arms that look great in sleeveless tops!

1 Stand with feet hip-width apart, stomach muscles pulled in and hands resting by your sides.

2 Extend your right arm out in front of you with your palm flat, facing the ceiling.

3 Extend your left arm, placing the left palm on top of the right palm. Gently push your hands against each other. You will feel the stretch in your biceps.

4 Hold for three sets of 10 seconds, then repeat for the other arm.

WATCH POINT
Don't try to force your hands together with a lot of pressure. Just take it slowly and start with a small amount of pressure in order to achieve a gentle stretch.

4

3

Tricep stretch

Your tricep muscles are found at the back of the top of your arms. Giving them a good stretch will boost circulation and help to get rid of any blotchy, pimply skin that may reside there.

1 Stand with feet hip-width apart. Lift your right arm above your head and bend your elbow so your hand drops down behind your neck.

2 Grip your right elbow with your left hand and pull it gently to the left – this will automatically force your right hand to dip down between your shoulder blades. You should feel the tricep muscle stretch in your right arm. Keep your chin lifted, so you don't put a strain on your neck.

3 Hold the stretch for two sets of 7 seconds then repeat the stretch, working your left arm instead.

WATCH POINT

This movement makes it really easy to let your head fall forwards so your chin is resting on your chest, but don't let this happen because it will put a strain on your neck. Keep your chin lifted and eyes forward throughout the stretch.

Seashell stretch

This stretch is great at targeting the muscles in your shoulders as well as your back. Just sit back and relax and you will feel the beneficial effects of the stretch.

1 Get down on the floor on your hands and knees. Sit back on to your calves, so your bottom is resting on your heels. Make sure your neck and head are relaxed and that you are looking down towards the floor.

2 Stretch your arms out in front of you so that your hands and fingertips are spread on the floor.

3 Walk your hands as far forwards as you can until you can feel the stretch in the middle of your back.

4 Hold the stretch for three sets of 10 seconds.

WATCH POINT

Don't strain your neck by trying to look in front of you – it's best to let your head and neck relax so you are looking down towards the floor.

1

3

Upper back stretch

Stretching out the muscles in the back will have a therapeutic effect on both your body and your state of mind. The back is one of the first areas to retain tension and stress, so stretching out the muscles will help to put you at ease and set you up for the day ahead.

1 Stand with feet hip-width apart. Interlink your fingers and push your hands out in front of you as far as possible. Your palms should be facing away from you.

2 Allow your upper back to relax by lowering your shoulders to their natural resting position.

3 Hold for 10 seconds. You should feel the stretch between your shoulder blades. Pause for a brief moment, then repeat the stretch twice more.

WATCH POINT
If you find it hard to get your back to relax, just take a deep breath and lower your shoulders. This will have an instant relaxing effect.

2

Knee squeezes

The Knee squeezes are a subtle way of stretching out the muscles across the middle of your back. This stretch feels very satisfying when done correctly, so spend some time making sure you get it right.

1 Lie on the floor with your knees bent and feet flat on the floor. Let your arms rest by your sides.

2 Gently bring your knees back towards your chest.

3 Engage your stomach muscles by pulling them in towards your spine and lift your tailbone ever so slightly off the floor. Grip your knees with your hands for support. You should feel a stretch across the middle of your back.

4 Hold the stretch for three sets of 10 seconds, taking a very brief pause in-between.

WATCH POINT

It's common to want to hold your breath during this stretch but make sure you don't. Breathe slowly and deeply and you will make the stretch easier to do and more effective.

BACK & NECK

Lower back stretch

This stretch is ideal for targeting the muscles across your lower back, which have a tendency to ache, especially if you've had a bad night's sleep. Stretching them in the morning will help to reduce your risk of injury during the day.

3

1 Stand with feet hip-width apart and knees slightly bent.

2 Place your hands on your inner thighs with your palms facing outwards.

3 Engage your abdominals and slowly arch your spine until you feel a stretch across your lower back.

4 Hold for around 8 seconds then slowly stretch up through the spine until you are back in a normal standing position. Keep your back straight, with your chin up and looking forwards.

5 Repeat the stretch three times.

WATCH POINT
If you're not feeling the stretch, simply move your palms further down your thighs — this should help to increase it.

Waist and lower spine

This is another great way of targeting your lower back muscles and really stretching them out. If you do it slowly and gently, it can even be good at soothing lower back problems.

2

1 Lie on the floor on your back with your legs straight out and your right arm extended out to the side.

2 Bending your right leg, grip your knee with your left hand and bring it over to your left-hand side so it gets as close to the floor as is comfortable. Keep your right hand extended out to your right-hand side because this will help to increase the stretch in your waist and lower spine.

3 Hold the stretch for two sets of 7 seconds with a brief pause between. Repeat on your right side.

WATCH POINT
When you are stretching to the left side, make sure you keep the right hip on the floor and vice versa. This will stop you from stretching too far over and putting a strain on your lower back.

Cat stretch

This stretch is known as the Cat stretch because you look a lot like a cat if you do it right! It targets most of the major muscles in the back.

1 Get down on the floor on all fours. Let your head and neck relax so they are in line with your spine and you are looking down towards the floor.

2 Slowly arch your back, by pulling in your tummy muscles and pushing the curve of your spine towards the ceiling. Tilt your head and neck up towards the ceiling as you do this.

3 Hold the stretch for around 8 seconds then lower your back so it's straight and in the starting position again. While you do this, let your head and neck relax also.

4 Pause for a brief moment then repeat three times.

5 When you have finished, lean back on to your heels and stretch your arms out in front of you – this completes the movement.

WATCH POINT
Try not to let your back sag because this could cause serious back injuries. You can avoid this by doing the stretch slowly and gently to make sure you are in control at all times.

2

5

Neck stretches

This is a great substitute for a neck massage. It really helps to get your muscles loose, warm and nicely stretched. Plus, it's much safer than rolling your neck, because it puts less of a strain on the surrounding muscles.

1 Stand up straight with feet hip-width apart. Relax your shoulders and look straight ahead of you.

2 Start the stretch by slowly lowering your chin to your chest. Hold for a few seconds while you feel the stretch across the back of your neck and then gently raise your head so it's back in the starting position.

3 Next, rotate your head to the right and hold for a few seconds, then rotate your head to the left. Hold for a few seconds then return to the start position so you are looking straight ahead.

4 Repeat the sequence three times, until the 30 seconds are up.

WATCH POINT
Make sure your hips are facing forwards at all times – it's just your head that's supposed to be rotating, not your entire body!

2

3

3

TWO-WEEK PLAN

This two-week plan is an example of the way you can structure your stretching regime. We've chosen a mixture of different stretches to target each of the major muscle groups in the body to give you a great all-over programme.

You'll do two sets of six stretches each morning to last for 6 minutes. If you want to draw up your own plan you can. However, we recommend you start with our plan and monitor your results – how flexible you become and how relaxed you feel – then you can adapt it if you need to. Now, let's get started...

Day 1

Seated hamstring stretch **p40**
Piriformis stretch **p46**
Runner's calf stretch **p50**
Push down **p54**
Easy chest stretch **p60**
Upper back stretch **p68**

Day 2

Inner thigh stretch **p41**
Seated gluteal stretch **p47**
Push-off calf stretch **p51**
Up and over **p55**
Front-lying chest lift **p61**
Knee squeezes **p69**

Day 3

Day 4

Day 5

Day 6

TWO-WEEK PLAN

Day 7

Seated hamstring stretch **p40**
Bend and stretch **p49**
Soleus stretch **p52**
Push down **p54**
Tricep stretch **p66**
Neck stretches **p73**

Day 9

Hip flexor stretch **p42**
Seated gluteal stretch **p47**
Soleus stretch **p52**
Twist **p56**
Seashell stretch **p67**
Knee squeezes **p69**

Day 8

Inner thigh stretch **p41**
Piriformis stretch **p46**
Point and flex stretch **p53**
Up and over **p55**
Easy chest stretch **p60**
Upper back stretch **p68**

Day 10

Quadriceps stretch **p43**
Cross and dip **p48**
Runner's calf stretch **p50**
Full body stretch **p57**
Front-lying chest lift **p61**
Lower back stretch **p70**

Day 11

Day 12

Day 13

Day 14

body toning

Toning your body will **increase** your
muscular strength
and **improve** your
overall physical fitness. Having a trim,
toned **physique** also makes you **look**

good and can do wonders
for your **self-confidence**.

INTRODUCTION

Having a trim, toned physique makes you strong and healthy looking. Plus, building a bit of muscle will boost your metabolic rate, so you'll burn more calories during the day and reduce the amount of fat that your body stores. A good body-toning regime is an excellent, low-impact way to exercise, and can be a great stress reliever, too.

The exercises in this section focus on the legs, buttocks, stomach, arms, chest and back, so each day you'll have a thorough workout. Some parts of the body, such as the buttocks and thighs, are harder to tone, which is why you'll find more exercises devoted to these areas in the two-week plan.

If you find any of the exercises difficult to do, you can replace them with something else and adapt the two-week plan. Similarly, if you feel your arms are toning up much faster than your legs, make a few substitutions and get back to it.

The benefits

When the two weeks are up, you may find that your clothes feel looser and that your muscles look more defined. How well you respond depends much on your body composition – if you naturally have more muscle mass, then you're likely to respond quicker. If you

want to look more toned in time for a special occasion, follow the 'boost your body toning' tips (right) alongside the exercise programme, because they will help you to achieve your goals.

Boost your body toning

Making small changes to your lifestyle and the way you eat can help boost the effects of the plan and maximize your results. Try the following tips for healthy eating and living, but remember to speak to a doctor or nutritionist before making changes to your diet.

• Cut down on saturated fat and refined sugar, found in convenience foods like cakes, biscuits, sweets and fast food. It sends your blood sugar skyrocketing, promotes cravings and will encourage you to overeat.

• Stick to pure, fresh foods such as vegetables, fruit and wholegrains. Combining lean protein with vegetables or salad at mealtimes will fuel the muscles and help you stay lean and strong.

• Drink up to eight glasses of water a day to help flush toxins out of your system, beat bloating and make the muscles work more effectively.

• Be more active – take the stairs instead of the lift and try to walk everywhere you can. It will seriously boost the number of calories you burn.

ENGAGE YOUR STOMACH MUSCLES

This is required for exercises that target your core stability (the muscles at the centre of your stomach). To engage your stomach muscles, simply pull them in towards your spine, making sure you keep breathing. Be careful not to arch your back. You'll now be in the perfect position to carry out the required exercises.

Effective toning

Some exercises in this section require you to repeat the movement until the full 30 seconds are up. We've given the suggested number of repetitions you should try, but just do as many as you can comfortably achieve in that time. To make it effective, it's important that you don't stop for more than a minute between exercises. Shorter recovery periods result in better muscles all round and improved muscle endurance. So keep going!

What you'll need

For this routine you'll need a non-slip mat, a set of dumbbells (or tins from the cupboard), a chair, a sturdy step (like the bottom of a staircase) and a towel. You'll also need to use a wall and a door handle for some exercises. Don't forget to warm up and cool down!

Squat

The Squat is one of the most effective exercises for toning the muscles in the legs and buttocks, including the hamstrings (at the back of the legs). Plus, it's a great way to build strength in the lower body. It's an easy exercise to get right and you can really feel it working.

1 Stand with feet hip-width apart. You can either place your hands on your hips or hold on to the back of a chair for support if needed.

2 Look straight ahead and count to three while you bend your knees and push your bottom out behind you, until you feel the muscles working in the backs of your thighs and buttocks. The deeper you can squat, the better it is for working those muscles, but make sure you keep your feet flat on the floor at all times. Keep your back straight and make sure your spine is in line with your head and neck.

3 Return to the starting position, counting to three as you go, and get ready to do it all over again!

Number of repetitions: Aim for around ten.

2

WATCH POINT
Make sure your feet remain flat on the floor. Don't let them rise up when you bend your knees.

Lying hip rotations

This exercise tones and strengthens the muscles in the hips, so is great for improving the appearance of the dreaded saddlebags (those annoying pockets of fat that can appear on the outside of the top of the thighs). By clenching your buttocks as you rotate your hip, you'll be giving them a workout too!

1 Lie on your left side, bending your left knee so it's at a 45-degree angle to your body.

2 Lift up and support your upper body with your left arm – this should be a comfortable resting position. Place your right hand on the floor in front of you for additional support.

3 Contract your buttocks and raise your right leg off the floor from the hip joint as far as you can, keeping the foot flexed (bent at the ankle).

WATCH POINT
Try and get your leg as high as you can without straining – you'll find it gets easier with practice.

3

4 Gently lower your leg out in front of you, down toward the floor so it's at a right angle to your body. Keep it as straight as you can without locking your knee.

5 Bring your right leg back into the starting position, keeping it just off the floor.

Number of repetitions: Do three or more repetitions on one side and then reverse the entire movement and do the same on the other.

4

Standing calf raises

The calf muscles are hard to target, although studies have shown that walking in high heels can help to tone them up! To get really sexy, shapely calves, we recommend you try this exercise instead.

1 Stand with both feet near the edge of a raised object such as a stair or a big chunky book. Place the ball of your right foot on the edge of the raised object, letting your heel extend off the edge.

2 Hold on to a wall or a chair for support and, lifting your left leg into the air slightly by bending at the knee, gently let your right heel drop down until you feel the stretch in your calf. Keep your back straight, your head up, and your right leg straight.

3 Rise up on to your right toe as high as you can and hold for a second while flexing the calf muscle.

4 Carefully return to the starting position, then repeat with the left leg.

Number of repetitions: Aim to do around ten on each foot.

2

WATCH POINT

Make sure that you don't slip off the raised object by carefully controlling the move. If that means you have to do fewer than ten reps on each foot during the 30 seconds, so be it.

Superman

You need to have a good sense of balance to do this exercise, so if you don't get it right first time, be patient. It's great for increasing core stability and endurance in the joints, as well as working the core muscles in your thighs.

1 Get down on the floor on all fours, then pull in your abdominal muscles.

2 Extend your right arm out in front of you and your left leg out behind you, keeping it as straight as you can without locking your elbow or knee. Engage your abdominal muscles to help stop your back from arching – it will reduce any risk of injury. You will feel the muscles working in the thigh of your extended leg. If you want to increase the effects, point your toes – it will make you tense your muscles even harder. Keep your head and neck in line with your back to make sure you're not twisting your neck.

3 Slowly return to the start position and repeat with the opposite leg and arm.

Number of repetitions: Beginners should hold the position for 12 seconds then swap, but if you feel comfortable, try moving your arm and leg in and out for extra toning effects.

WATCH POINT
Do this on soft carpet or a padded exercise mat, so you don't hurt your knees.

Step-back lunge

This exercise will help to tone the quadriceps (known as the quad muscles) at the front of your thighs to give you a healthy and athletic look.

1 Stand with feet hip-width apart and rest your hands on your hips.

2 Keep your right foot firmly on the floor and lunge backwards with your left leg, bending your knee until it rests around 15 cm (6 inches) above the floor. You should be balancing on the ball of your left foot, and will be able to feel the muscles working in the front of the left thigh.

3 Return to the starting position, then repeat with the other leg.

Number of repetitions: Aim to do around three on each leg, or more if you feel comfortable.

WATCH POINT

Check behind you to make sure you have enough room to step back into the lunge. If you want to make the exercise more demanding, you can hold dumbbells as you do it.

1

2

Side kick

The Side kick is an energetic exercise that will get your heart rate pumping and really burn some calories. It's great for toning the hamstrings and quads and it will give your waist a workout too.

1 Stand with feet hip-width apart. Bring your hands up to your chest and form loose fists, while keeping your elbows bent and by your sides to help you balance.

2 Raise your right leg off the floor and kick it out to the side in a swift, controlled move. Be careful not to flick your leg, as you could jar your knee or hip.

3 Bring your leg back to the starting position and repeat the movement for 30 seconds.

4 Repeat the movement with your left leg.

Number of repetitions: Aim to do around ten on each leg.

1

2

WATCH POINT
Be careful that you don't use too much force to shoot your leg out to the side or you may end up straining a muscle or jarring your knee.

Rear leg raise

This exercise will help to strengthen and tone both the gluteus maximus (the major muscles in the buttocks, which are also known as the glutes) and also the lower back.

1 Lie on the floor with your forehead resting on the backs of your hands. Make sure your spine is in line with your neck.

2 Squeeze your buttocks – it will make the exercise harder and more effective. Then, engage your abdominal muscles and gently lift your right leg off the floor until you feel the muscles working in your buttocks. Keep your leg straight and your knee soft. You shouldn't feel any pain in your lower back.

3 Lower your right leg back into the starting position then repeat the movement with your left leg and again with your right and so on until the 30 seconds are up.

Number of repetitions: Aim to complete around three sets of ten. You can do five sets of six with a slight pause between if you prefer.

WATCH POINT
Don't try to lift your leg too high or it will force your back to arch and put a strain on the muscles.

Lunge

This is different from the Step-back lunge, which works the muscles in the legs, because shifting your core body weight to the front means that the muscles in your buttocks will bear most of the brunt. Lunging is great for strengthening as well as toning the muscles and is a firm favourite among personal fitness trainers.

1 Stand with feet hip-width apart. Rest your hands on your hips or by your sides.

2 Step forwards with your right leg, bending your knee so your thigh is almost at a right-angle to the floor. Your right foot should be flat on the floor. Your left leg should be slightly bent at the knee and the ball of your left foot should be resting on the floor behind you, with your heel slightly in the air.

3 Hold for a second, then push off the floor with your right foot and return to the starting position.

4 Repeat the movement with alternate legs until the 30 seconds are up.

Number of repetitions: Aim to do around ten lunges (five on each side) in the allotted time.

WATCH POINT
Don't rush the lunge or go down too far or you'll end up banging your knee on the floor. Always make sure you go at your own pace.

2

Crane stand

This exercise is like the Superman, but standing up. It's great for working your buttocks, hamstrings and lower back but it does take a lot of skill and balance to achieve, so do it slowly for best results.

1 Stand on your left leg and take a few seconds to find your balance.

2 Extend your left arm out in front of you and your right leg out behind you. Try to keep your right leg as straight as possible without locking the knee.

3 Reach out as far as possible and tilt your body over from the waist so your left arm drops down to the floor.

4 Gently straighten up from the waist so you're back in the starting position. Repeat with the opposite arm and leg.

2

3

Number of repetitions: Aim to do around four, or more if you feel comfortable.

WATCH POINT
This exercise is suitable for everyone. Just concentrate and take it slowly to make sure you keep your balance.

Stiff-legged touchdown

This exercise takes a bit of skill and balance to execute, but the results are worth it. Stretching down to touch your toes from a standing position will work all the supporting muscles around your buttocks and thighs and help improve your core stability. It's similar to the Crane stand, but you are bending from the waist.

1 Stand with feet hip-width apart. Rest your hands on your hips or by your side. Lift your right leg off the floor and take a second to find your balance. You may need to rest the tips of your toes on the floor if you feel you are about to topple over.

2 Reach down and try to touch the toes of your 'stiff' (straight) left leg with your left arm. Make sure that you keep your left leg straight and your knee soft.

3 At the same time, extend your right leg backwards (don't lock the knee). Raise your right arm for balance. If you can't reach your toes, let your hand hover in the air as far down as is comfortable.

4 Slowly return to the starting position and repeat with the other leg.

Number of repetitions: Hold the pose for around 10 seconds, then repeat with the other leg.

1

2

3

Side-step squat

This exercise is an 80s aerobics classic, which is so effective that it's still used today in most good fitness routines. Squatting to the side targets all the muscles along the inner thigh and bottom to help sculpt a beautiful-looking rear view.

1 Stand feet hip-width apart, with your feet slightly turned out and flat on the floor. Rest your hands on your hips or by your sides.

2 Step your right leg out to the side and bend your right knee, so you lower yourself by a few centimetres (several inches) towards the floor. Let your full body weight fall onto your right leg. Keep both feet firmly on the floor at all times.

3 Push off from the floor with your right foot and return to the starting position.

4 Repeat the movement with your left leg and keep repeating the exercise on alternate legs until the 30 seconds are up.

Number of repetitions: Aim to do around ten Side-step squats on each leg.

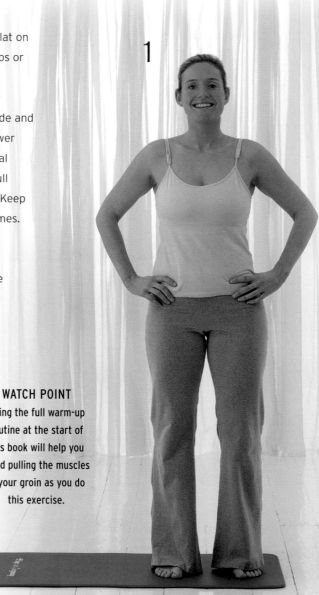

WATCH POINT
Doing the full warm-up routine at the start of this book will help you avoid pulling the muscles in your groin as you do this exercise.

Stepping

This is a great exercise if you like 'feeling the burn'. Stepping up on to a stair forces the glutes (the muscles in the buttocks) to squeeze and contract, so will help create a pert bottom.

1 Stand at the bottom of the stairs or in front of a big chunky book. Rest your hands on your hips or let them rest by your side.

2 Step up on to the step with your left leg and let your right leg follow.

3 Step down off the step with your left leg and let the right leg follow.

4 Repeat, starting with the right leg.

Number of repetitions: You should be able to manage around 15 or more during the 30 seconds.

WATCH POINT
Do this barefoot or wear a good pair of sports trainers rather than slippery socks for this exercise so that you don't slip off the step. Plus, don't rush the move.

Reverse curl

This is great for targeting the stomach muscles. You should feel it really working all across your stomach – the harder you concentrate, the more effective it will be.

1 Lie on the floor, making sure that the small of your back is pressed against the floor and not arching upwards. An easy way to do this is to engage your abdominal muscles so you feel them contract.

2 Bring your knees toward your chest and cross your feet at the ankles. Rest your hands by your sides on the floor for support.

3 In one carefully controlled move, use your stomach muscles to lift your bottom and lower back off the floor. Aim to straighten your feet and knees and push them up towards the ceiling. You don't have to move far, just enough to feel your muscles working.

4 Count to two on the way up and two on the way down.

5 When you've done 30 seconds' worth of repetitions, place your feet back on the floor. Return to your starting position.

Number of repetitions: Aim to do around seven during the 30 seconds.

WATCH POINT

Make sure you're lying on soft carpet or a padded exercise mat to reduce the risk of bruising your spine. If you're a complete beginner, a slightly easier version of the Reverse curl is to use your stomach muscles to bring your knees further in toward your chest rather than up toward the ceiling.

Plank

This doesn't sound or look too taxing but, if you do it right, you'll find that it's one of the most intense exercises in the book, and very effective at toning the abdominal muscles. Many people, especially beginners, find this difficult to hold for long periods of time, so see how you get on. Aim to hold for the full 30 seconds by the end of two weeks.

1 Lie on the floor on your front, resting your forehead on the backs of your hands.

2 Keeping your elbows bent, slide your hands across the floor, rotating from the shoulders, until you find your perfect 'press-up' position either side of your chest.

3 Curl your toes underneath you and push up off the floor with your hands. Keep your elbows soft to stop them locking, and keep your neck and head relaxed and in line with your spine.

4 Hold the pose for 10 seconds, then gently lower yourself back down to the floor again. Remember to breathe during the exercise.

Number of repetitions: Start by doing three sets of 10 seconds. Try to increase the time that you hold the Plank to the full 30 seconds by the end of two weeks.

WATCH POINT
This exercise can be difficult to do so don't over-strain yourself — you may be able to hold the position for only five seconds at first. Just persevere!

2

3

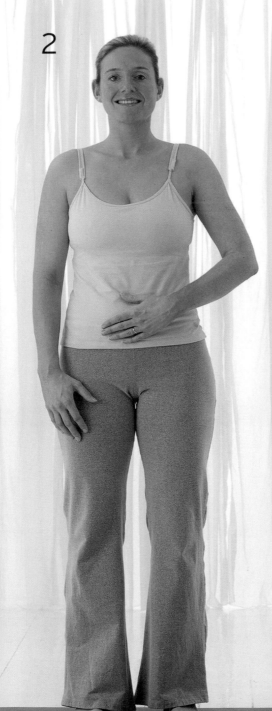

2

Stomach tuck-in

This exercise is like the natural alternative to wearing a corset. It works the deep muscles in your stomach – the transverse abdominals – to help flatten and define the muscles. It's the perfect start to getting a super-flat stomach.

1 Stand with feet hip-width apart and hands resting by your sides.

2 Slowly contract your abdominals (your stomach muscles) by pulling them in toward your spine, but don't hold your breath. If you put your hand to your stomach you should feel the muscles tighten – this means they're working. For best results, really concentrate on what you're doing and how it feels.

3 Slowly release and get ready to start again.

Number of repetitions: Hold for 10 seconds and repeat three times.

WATCH POINT
This exercise can also be done sitting on a chair.

Waist twist

Make sure you have a lot of space around you so that when you swing your arms you don't hit anything. This is a fun exercise to do and it really gets to work on the obliques (the muscles at the side of your waist), to help define a curvy silhouette.

1 Stand with feet hip-width apart, hands by sides, and knees slightly bent.

2 Extend your arms out in front of you and form loose fists with both hands.

3 Swing your arms from side to side, making sure your feet stay firmly on the floor, and your hips face forward. Start off slowly and then build up speed, making sure you keep control of the movement and your hips stay facing the front.

4 When the 30 seconds are up, drop your arms back down by your sides and return to the starting position.

Number of repetitions: Do as many as you can in the 30 seconds.

WATCH POINT

Don't get carried away while swinging your arms as you may end up pulling a muscle. If you have to go slowly to control the movement, so be it.

3

Crunches

This is an intense workout for your stomach muscles and a great way of getting a washboard-flat tum.

1 Lie on the floor, knees bent and feet (apart) flat on the floor in line with your hips. Make sure your lower back is pressed into the floor. Put your hands behind your head to support your neck.

2 Engage your stomach muscles, by pulling your abdominals towards your spine, and lift your upper body off the floor as far as you can without arching your lower back. You may find that you can't get up very high, but it's the effort of moving that counts, so make sure that you're pushing yourself as hard as you comfortably can. With practice, you may be able to sit up completely.

3 When you can't go any further, pause for 1 second. Then gently lower yourself back down into the starting position and repeat.

Number of repetitions: Try to do as many sets of five as possible, with a brief rest between. By the end of two weeks you should aim to do the Crunches continuously for 30 seconds.

WATCH POINT

Make sure you don't use your neck to pull yourself up or you'll feel the strain the next day. Supporting your neck with your hands will prevent this, but don't use your hands to lift your head off the floor – let your stomach muscles do all the work.

1

3

Bicycle

This is similar to the Crunches exercise, but crossing your elbow to the opposite knee targets the obliques instead, which are found at the side of the waist. Practising this exercise will help give you a smaller, more defined middle.

1 Lie on the floor with your knees bent and feet flat on the floor.

2 Rest your hands behind your head and, using your stomach muscles, lift your upper body off the floor, making sure that your lower back stays firmly on the floor.

3 Lift your right foot off the floor and bring your right knee towards your chest.

4 Reach forwards and rotate from the waist slightly in order to bring your left elbow towards your right knee. They don't have to touch.

5 Pause for one second then return to the starting position. Repeat the movement, bringing your right knee towards your left elbow.

6 Continue the exercise on alternate sides until the 30 seconds are up.

Number of repetitions: Aim to do as many as you can in the 30 seconds - around 12. Take a brief pause if you have to, for example, between sets of six.

WATCH POINT
Make sure your head and neck are in line with your spine and that you're looking up toward the ceiling – it will prevent you from straining your neck.

3

4

ARMS

Press-ups

This is a good all-round exercise for toning the major muscles in the arms. It's really good for developing upper-body strength and balancing out a pear-shaped figure.

1 Lie face-down on the floor, with your forehead resting on the backs of your hands. Slide your hands around to rest at shoulder level, to find your ideal 'press-up' position either side of your chest.

2 Use your arms to lift your upper body off the floor and bring your knees in towards your chest a little so they're resting on the floor, taking most of your body weight. Cross your feet at the ankles and raise them off the floor slightly. This should automatically cause your body weight to shift back on to your arms.

3 Bend your elbows and gently lower your upper body back down to the floor, keeping your head and shoulders level and in line with your spine at all times. Then push off the floor with your hands, raising your upper body into the air. Aim to get your arms straight, while keeping your elbows soft. Repeat this movement.

Number of repetitions: Aim for two sets of 10 during the 30 seconds.

WATCH POINT

Engaging your tummy muscles will help keep your back straight and reduce any risk of injury. When the Press-up becomes easier to do, extend your legs fully out behind you and curl your toes under so they remain on the floor instead of your knees when you push up.

2

3

Bicep curl

The biceps are the muscles at the front of the upper arms. They are relatively easy to tone, so practising this exercise will help give you shapely arms that you'll want to show off.

1 Stand up tall with feet hip-width apart and knees soft.

2 Extend your arms out in front of you with palms facing upwards, holding a tin of soup or a dumbbell in each hand.

3 Bend your elbows and bring both your hands in towards your shoulders so that your arms form right-angles.

4 Reverse the movement so that your elbows are fully extended in front of you again. Keep your elbows soft at all times.

5 Repeat the movement until the 30 seconds are up.

Number of repetitions: Aim to do as many as you can during the time period without rushing.

Tricep extension

The triceps are the muscles at the back of the upper arms. If they're left to slack, it can lead to the dreaded 'bingo wing' effect, where loose skin on the underside of your arm wobbles as you wave. It's classically a hard muscle to target, but this exercise will help to tighten and tone.

1 Stand with feet hip-width apart. Pick up a heavy object with both hands – choose something that you can work comfortably with, such as a dumbbell or a heavy book.

2 Bring the object over your head with straight arms.

3 Bend your arms at the elbows, so you slowly lower it down between your shoulder blades.

4 Reverse the movement by straightening your arms so you bring the object directly back above your head.

5 Repeat Steps 3 and 4 slowly, so you're in control of the movement.

Number of repetitions: Aim to do around seven in the 30 seconds.

WATCH POINT
Choose a weight that's challenging but not so heavy that you can't control it – you don't want to end up dropping it on your head.

Bench dip

As well as working your triceps, this will help improve your core stability and tone up your tummy. It's especially great for the arms because you're using your body weight to strengthen and tone.

1 Sit on the edge of a chair with your hands resting either side of your bottom, gripping the edge of the seat.

2 Walk your feet away from the chair as far as you can so your bottom comes off the edge of the chair.

3 Letting your arms take your body weight, bend your elbows and, with knees bent, slowly lower your body towards the floor – make sure you don't end up sitting on the floor; hovering just above the floor is the ideal position. Make sure your weight is evenly distributed so you don't topple the chair.

4 Straighten your arms, so you bring your lower body back up. Repeat Steps 3 and 4.

Number of repetitions: Aim for around six.

WATCH POINT
Keep your forearms vertical at all times –
it will help to reduce the amount of strain on
your shoulders.

ARMS

Tricep kick-back

This is another great exercise that will help to banish bingo wings and tone up those hard-to-target tricep muscles at the back of the upper arms. When you do this exercise, make sure that your arm extends directly out behind you rather than veering off to the side.

1

3 Bend your left elbow and bring the dumbbell back to the start position, next to your shoulder.

4 Repeat around 12 times and then swap your position so you're doing the exercise with the right arm.

Number of repetitions: Do around 10–12 with one arm, then swap to work the other.

WATCH POINT
Be careful not to swing your arm while doing the movement – you'll get better results if you do it more slowly and stay in control.

2

1 Grab yourself a chair and rest your right hand and right knee on the seat. Keep your left leg straight with your knee soft and hold a dumbbell or tin of soup in your left hand.

2 Bend your left elbow and bring your left hand up to shoulder height, then 'kickback' with your left arm so it's fully extended out behind you. Although we call it a kickback, you should carry out the movement in a slow and controlled manner.

Circles in the air

This exercise is great for general toning of the arms and shoulders. Using weights will also help to develop strength in the arms and have a pumping effect on the muscles, so you'll look great in short-sleeved tops.

1 Stand with feet hip-width apart, knees slightly bent and arms resting by your sides.

2 With a dumbbell in each hand, cross your arms in front of each other level with your hips, then circle them up towards the ceiling so they cross over in the air above your head. Then bring them back round to the starting position.

3 Pause for one second then repeat the movement in the opposite direction.

Number of repetitions: Aim to do around 15 in the 30 seconds.

WATCH POINT
Keep your arms fully extended as you circle them so you are working as many muscles as possible, but remember to keep your elbows soft.

2

2

2

Reverse sit-up

This is a great exercise for strengthening the lower back. Adding an arm rotation to the move delivers a double toning boost to the shoulders.

1 Lie flat and face down on the floor with your forehead resting on the backs of your hands.

2 Squeeze your buttocks and use your stomach muscles to raise your chest off the floor as far as you feel comfortable.

1

3 Squeeze your shoulder blades together by rotating your arms around from the shoulders so your palms are facing downwards and your forearms are hovering at chest level. This will help to give the shoulders a workout, too.

4 Return your arms to the starting position and lower your chest back down to the floor. Repeat the movement.

Number of repetitions: Aim to do around 15 or more during the 30 seconds.

WATCH POINT
Don't try to pull your chest back too far or it will force your lower back to arch and put a strain on the muscles. Just do what feels comfortable.

3

Moy complex

This exercise is also known as the 'row, rotate and press' and is a great way to tone the muscles in your back, without having to use the complicated machinery that you find in the gym.

1 Sit on the edge of a chair with a dumbbell or tin of soup in each hand.

2 Bend over from the waist so your chest is resting on your knees. Make sure your head and neck are relaxed, so that you're looking down towards the floor.

3 Start with your hands resting on the floor, with elbows slightly bent, then bend your arms and bring your hands up to shoulder level.

4 Rotate your wrists and extend your arms out in front of you so that they're parallel to the floor.

5 Retrace your steps so you're back in the Step 2 position, then repeat the movement.

Number of repetitions: Aim to do around 15 repetitions during the 30 seconds.

WATCH POINT
Remember to relax your head and neck and keep them in line with your spine, so you don't strain any muscles.

Dumbbell row

Doing this exercise is like starting a lawnmower. It targets the muscles in the middle of the back, such as the trapezius. So, if you practise this religiously, it will make wearing backless dresses all the more appealing.

1 Rest your right knee and your right hand on the seat of a chair, like you do for the Tricep kick-back.

2 Holding a dumbbell or tin of soup in your left hand, pull it back towards your hip.

3 Extend your left arm diagonally out in front of you, so it travels towards the ground.

4 Bring the dumbbell back to your hip and repeat the movement.

Number of repetitions: Aim to do around 10–12 on your left arm before swapping your position so you're working your right arm for the remainder of the 30 seconds.

WATCH POINT
You should do this exercise on one side at a time if you have a bad back. If you want to work both sides at once, take away the chair and stand in a squat position while doing the exercise.

2

3

Doorknob pull-up

It sounds strange, but this is a perfect exercise to do at home. As you lean back, the resistance created by holding the towel around the doorknobs will give all the muscles in your back a good workout.

1 Open a suitable door and wrap a hand towel around both the doorknobs.

2 Making sure it's secure, drop down into a squat position, holding one end of the towel in each hand. You should be leaning back from the waist, taking the slack from the towel so you feel the muscles working in your back.

WATCH POINT

Don't rush this exercise. You'll feel a greater resistance if you do it slowly and carefully rather than trying to fit as many as possible into the 30 seconds.

3

3 Hold for a few seconds then pull yourself back up to a standing position and repeat the movement.

Number of repetitions: Try to do around 20 in the 30 seconds.

Wall push-up

This is like a standing press-up and is great for toning the muscles in the chest, especially the pectoral muscles (known as the pecs), which can be found underneath your bust. If you master the move, it will help you to achieve a perky bust without having to resort to surgery!

WATCH POINT
Make sure you really put some effort into pushing off from the wall – that way it will work your arms as well as your chest.

1 Stand around two feet away from the wall with feet hip-width apart and legs straight. Make sure your knees are soft.

2 Lean forwards and place your palms flat against the wall.

3 Bend your arms at the elbows and bring your chest towards the wall.

4 Squeeze the muscles in your chest and push off from the wall so you are standing back in the start position.

Number of repetitions: Aim for around 15 during the 30 seconds.

3

Prayer

This is excellent for toning the pectoral muscles (the pecs). Like the Wall push-up exercise, toning these muscles will help to give you a more youthful-looking bust.

1 Either while standing or sitting, press the palms of your hands together at shoulder height while extending your elbows out to the sides.

2 Hold the pose for as long as you can – ideally around 10 seconds, pressing your palms together with as much force as you feel comfortable with. Take one second to rest and then repeat the pose until the 30 seconds are up.

Number of repetitions: Aim to hold the pose for 10 seconds and then take 1 second to rest and start again. By the end of two weeks you should aim to hold the pose for the full 30 seconds.

WATCH POINT
Many people will find their joints crack when doing this exercise, so start by pressing the palms lightly together and gradually start to build up the pressure. Doing the exercise this way will help prevent you from getting cramp.

1

Fly

The weights used in this exercise will give the muscles in your chest an extra toning boost and help to build strength in the arms too. It's a great all-round upper body workout.

1 Lie on the floor on your back and hold a dumbbell or tin of soup in each hand. Bend your knees and place your feet flat on the floor.

2 Extend both arms at a right angle to your body so that you're in a crucifix position.

3 Keeping your arms straight, with elbows soft, gently lift them above your head so that you bring the dumbbells together.

4 Pause for a second then gently lower arms back to the floor to the start position. Repeat.

Number of repetitions: Aim to do around three, then pause for a few seconds and repeat until the 30 seconds are up.

WATCH POINT
Make sure your arms are not bent – keep your elbows soft throughout the exercise.

2

3

Soup-tin press

This exercise is great for toning the muscles in your chest and around your collarbone to help give you a slinky look. Make it a priority if you're aiming to squeeze into a strapless dress in two weeks.

1 Lie on your back, with your knees bent and feet flat on the floor, holding a dumbbell or tin of soup in each hand.

2 Bend your elbows and rest your hands by your armpits, so they're hovering just above your shoulders.

3 Extend your arms into the air at a right angle to your body, holding the dumbbells directly over your shoulders with your palms facing away from you.

4 Pull in your abdominals and tilt your chin towards your chest.

5 Release your chin, then bend your elbows and bring your hands back to the starting position. Pause for one second then repeat.

Number of repetitions: Aim to do around 15.

WATCH POINT

Push from the shoulders as you extend your arms, for maximum effects. Plus, make sure your lower back is pushed into the floor all the time throughout this exercise.

2

3

TWO-WEEK PLAN

This two-week plan is an example of the way you can structure your exercise regime. We've chosen exercises to target each of the major muscle groups in the body to give you a great all-over workout.

Each morning you will start with a brief warm-up. We've picked six different exercises each day to create a 3-minute routine, which should be carried out twice to make the workout last a total of 6 minutes.

You can easily draw up your own plan if you want to. Make sure you include a good mix of exercises but, if you want to aim for weight loss as well as toning, remember that the standing exercises will burn a lot more calories than the others. Plus, any exercise that targets the legs is going to create a big calorie expenditure. Only you can know your body's major trouble zones, so can include extra exercises to target those particular areas.

We recommend you start with our plan and monitor your results. If you choose to do the two-week plan again at some point in the future, that's when you can start to adjust it if you wish. Now, let's get started.

Day 1

Squat **p82**
Side kick **p87**
Rear leg raise **p88**
Reverse curl **p94**
Press-ups **p100**
Reverse sit-up **p106**

Day 2

Lying hip rotations **p83**
Lunge **p89**
Stepping **p93**
Plank **p95**
Bicep curl **p101**
Moy complex **p107**

Day 3

Standing calf raises **p84**
Crane stand **p90**
Stomach tuck-in **p96**
Bicycle **p99**
Tricep extension **p102**
Dumbbell row **p108**

Day 5

Step-back lunge **p86**
Side-step squat **p92**
Crunches **p98**
Tricep kick-back **p104**
Wall push-up **p110**
Soup-tin press **p113**

Day 4

Superman **p85**
Stiff-legged touchdown **p91**
Waist twist **p97**
Bench dip **p103**
Circles in the air **p105**
Doorknob pull-up **p109**

Day 6

Step-back lunge **p86**
Side kick **p87**
Stepping **p93**
Bicycle **p99**
Circles in the air **p105**
Prayer **p111**

TWO-WEEK PLAN

Day 7

Squat **p82**
Rear leg raise **p88**
Side-step squat **p92**
Reverse curl **p94**
Press-ups **p100**
Fly **p112**

Day 8

Lying hip rotations **p83**
Lunge **p89**
Plank **p95**
Crunches **p98**
Bicep curl **p101**
Soup-tin press **p113**

Day 9

Standing calf raises **p84**
Crane stand **p90**
Stomach tuck-in **p96**
Tricep extension **p102**
Tricep kick-back **p104**
Reverse sit-up **p106**

Day 10

Superman **p85**
Stiff-legged touchdown **p91**
Waist twist **p97**
Bench dip **p103**
Moy complex **p107**
Fly **p112**

Day 11

Standing calf raises **p84**
Step-back lunge **p86**
Side-step squat **p92**
Crunches **p98**
Tricep kick-back **p104**
Dumbbell row **p108**

Day 12

Step-back lunge **p86**
Stiff-legged touchdown **p91**
Side-step squat **p92**
Crunches **p98**
Tricep kick-back **p104**
Dumbbell row **p108**

Day 13

Side kick **p87**
Stepping **p93**
Waist twist **p97**
Bicycle **p99**
Circles in the air **p105**
Doorknob pull-up **p109**

Day 14

Squat **p82**
Rear leg raise **p88**
Reverse curl **p94**
Press-ups **p100**
Bench dip **p103**
Wall push-up **p110**

Toning up your stomach muscles improves your posture and helps protect your back from injury. A flat stomach is also flattering and will enhance your figure, whatever you choose to wear.

flat stomach

INTRODUCTION

Most of us would love to have a flatter stomach but just can't face the thought of hours of strenuous sit-ups. But the key to a flatter stomach is to exercise little and often. Doing the quick, easy routines in this section will give you a flatter stomach in two weeks.

The benefits

Apart from the obvious benefit of improving your appearance, firming and toning up your stomach muscles will improve your posture and balance, and increase your flexibility. Building muscle tone doesn't happen overnight, but the beauty of this short routine is that you won't become bored or burned out. Keep it up and you'll have a tighter tum in two weeks.

Effective exercising

Some exercises in this section require you to repeat the movement until the full 30 seconds are up. Just do as many reps as you can comfortably achieve in that time. To make it effective, it's important that you don't stop for more than a minute between exercises. Shorter recovery periods result in better muscles all round and improved muscle endurance. So keep going!

What you'll need

For this section you'll need a chair, a non-slip mat, a cushion, and a pillow or towel to support your head and neck.

Don't forget to warm up and cool down!

Eating for a flat stomach

Adopting a few healthy eating tips can help beat bloating and boost the effects of exercise.

Don't ever skimp on liquids if you think it could ward off bloating because drinking lots of water actually promotes a flat stomach by flushing toxins from your system and curbing your

appetite. If your body feels starved of water then it will hold on to what there is, which can lead to water retention and the appearance of bloating.

Drink at least eight glasses a day, but don't drink a lot before exercise because it will put pressure on your bladder. You'll know you're

well hydrated by checking the colour of your urine – the paler it is, the better.

If your stomach has a noticeable wobble, you will have to do some regular cardiovascular exercise to promote fat loss and these healthy eating tips will also help:

• Eat little and often and make sure you have a varied diet. Keep wheat products to a minimum because they can cause bloating and wind in people sensitive to wheat or gluten.

• Say goodbye to fizzy drinks – even if they're 'diet' or caffeine-free, they can still cause bloating because they are loaded with gassy bubbles.

• Avoid processed food and ready meals. They are usually laden with salt, sugar and chemicals, and can upset your stomach's bacterial balance and cause bloating.

• Cut down on salt – it can encourage fluid retention.

KEEPING YOUR SPINE IN NEUTRAL

This is the correct position for your spine during exercise. Lie down on your back, flat on the floor with your knees slightly bent and feet hip-width apart. Place your thumbs on your bottom ribs and your little fingers on the top of the hip bones. Draw these two points together by gently pulling your navel towards the floor to tighten your abdominal muscles. Keep your back in contact with the floor and do not arch your spine.

Stomach muscles explained

It helps to have a basic understanding of which muscles you need to work on to make your stomach appear flatter.

There are four abdominal muscle groups, which form a natural corset around the middle. They support your lower back, protect internal organs, and enable you to bend, twist and sit up. The deepest of the abdominal muscles is the transversus abdominis, which wraps horizontally around your waist and keeps your lower back stable. The rectus abdominis runs from the pubic bone to the bottom of the ribcage. This muscle enables your trunk to bend and is important for maintaining your posture.

The external and internal obliques run up the sides of your body and enable you to bend to the side and twist your spine. The exercises in this section will work to strengthen all these muscles for a firmer, flatter, fabulously toned stomach.

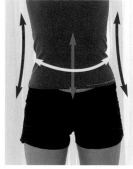

SEATED EXERCISES

These easy exercises can be performed when you're sitting at your desk or even when travelling. They're great for a quick tummy-toning session and for postural realignment. You'll need a straight-backed, sturdy chair – not one on castors.

Seated stomach workout

This tones and flattens your deep stomach muscle (transversus abdominis) and the one that runs down the front of your stomach (the rectus abdominis).

1 Sit forwards on a chair. Keep your feet flat on the floor, hip-width apart, with your knees over your ankles and your palms on your thighs.

2 Sit up straight. Tighten the abdominal muscles by gently pulling your navel in towards your spine. Hold for 10 seconds, then relax.

3 Rest for a count of three before doing any repetitions.

1

WATCH POINT
Remember to breathe regularly as you do this exercise – don't hold your breath because it will make your blood pressure rise, which can be dangerous when exercising.

2

WATCH POINT

Breathe normally throughout this exercise.

Mind over matter

Get the most from your workout by focusing on what you are doing as you are exercising, and tell yourself how well you are doing. You can even use visualizations as you exercise to convince yourself that your body is becoming fitter and more toned!

Hip hitch

This strengthens the oblique abdominal muscles and helps to stabilize your pelvis. This exercise is perfectly safe to do during pregnancy.

1 Sit with good posture with your hands resting on your thighs. Extend upwards through your spine.

2 Lift one hip towards your ribs, hold for a count of ten then release. Repeat on the other side.

Sitting pretty

If you sit properly, not only will those concertina-rolls of flesh diminish but you'll be doing your back a favour, too! Sit up straight with both feet on the floor, hip-width apart, and with your knees directly over your feet (don't tuck your feet under the chair). Try not to slump backwards or forwards because you'll put pressure on your lower back. Avoid crossing your legs, because this pushes your spine out of alignment. Tighten your abdominal muscles by gently pulling in your navel towards your backbone. Relax your shoulders and gently squeeze your shoulder blades together to stop them from rounding. Make this second nature and you'll soon notice the difference – you'll be able to breathe more deeply because your abdomen won't be squashed.

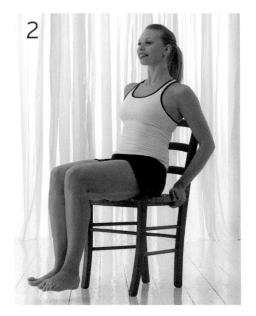

Seated knee lift

This seated exercise will work your rectus abdominis – the muscle that runs down the front of your stomach. Make sure your movements are controlled and flowing.

1 Sit on the edge of a chair with your knees bent and pressed together and your feet flat on the floor. Hold on to the sides of the chair, then tighten your stomach muscles.

2 Lean back slightly and lift your feet a few centimetres off the ground, keeping your knees bent and pressed together.

3 Slowly pull your knees in towards your chest and curl your upper body forwards. Then lower your feet to the floor. Rest for a count of three before you do any repetitions.

Controlling your movements

Make sure that all exercises are performed slowly, carefully, and with your full attention. You really do need to concentrate on what you're doing and think about how your body is responding to any exercise. If an action hurts or you do it quickly, then you're not doing it properly. Movements should flow in a gentle, controlled manner. This enables your muscles to stretch naturally.

WATCH POINT
Don't lean too far forwards or
you'll fall off the chair!

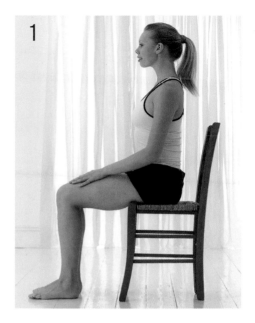

Spine rotation

This exercise gently mobilizes your spine, preparing it for harder exercises to come.

1 Sit forwards on a chair with your back straight and your hands resting on your thighs. Your knees should be over your ankles.

2 Tighten your abdominal muscles. Keeping your hips and knees forwards, slowly rotate your upper body to the left until you can put both hands on the back of the chair. Hold for a count of ten then return to the centre. Repeat the exercise, twisting to the right.

Don't exercise if...

- You are feeling unwell – your body will need all its strength to fight off any infection.
- You have an injury – you might make things worse.
- You have an ongoing medical condition or are on medication – consult with your doctor first.
- You've just had a big meal.
- You've been drinking alcohol.

WATCH POINT
Twist only as far as is comfortable.

Exercising in this position means you are working against gravity, making your muscles work even harder. Remember to keep your elbows soft, not locked.

Belly tightener

This is also known as abdominal hollowing and helps to shorten the abdominal muscles, which is good for your posture and creates the appearance of a flatter stomach.

WATCH POINT
Pull up the abdomen by using your deep abdominal muscles, not by arching your spine.

1 Kneel down on all fours (the 'box' position) with your hands shoulder-width apart, your elbows slightly bent and your knees under your hips. Keep your head in line with the rest of your body and look down at the floor, making sure that your chin isn't tucked into your chest.

2 Relax your abdominal muscles then slowly draw in your navel towards your spine.

3 Hold the muscles in for a count of ten then slowly relax. Breathe slowly and steadily throughout this exercise.

Easy plank (tension hold)

Holding your body in a three-quarters plank shape strengthens the deep transverse muscles that cross the stomach area. Keeping your knees on the floor makes this exercise much easier than the traditional plank, which you can progress to when you feel ready.

1 Adopt a traditional press-up position but keep your knees on the floor and your feet in the air. Your fingers should point forwards, your elbows stay straight but not locked, your head should be in line with your body and your feet together. Keep your shoulder blades drawn into your back and make sure you don't dip in the middle or raise your bottom in the air.

2 Hold this position for a count of ten, breathing regularly throughout.

How to breathe properly

Breathing is something we all take for granted but most of us only ever use the top third of our lungs. Learn to breathe properly and it's probably the best thing you can do for your overall health, because oxygen nourishes and replenishes all your body's cells. Abdominal breathing is a technique that enables you to breathe more deeply. It uses the diaphragm, the sheet of muscle forming the top of the abdomen, to help the lungs inflate and deflate effortlessly. Breathe in slowly through your nose, and notice how the top of the abdomen rises as you do so. Hold the breath for a few seconds, then breathe out slowly through your mouth.

WATCH POINT
Avoid this exercise if you have shoulder problems. If you feel any strain in your back muscles, move your knees further apart.

1

PELVIC TILTS

These exercises tighten the abdominal muscles without putting any strain on your back. They're a simple way to tone and strengthen your abdominal area.

Simple pelvic tilt

This easy exercise is particularly good if you're trying to shape up post-pregnancy.

1 Lie on your back with your knees bent and feet flat on the floor, hip-width apart, and your spine in neutral (see page 121). Rest your arms by your sides, with your palms facing the floor, and tighten your abdominal muscles.

2 Press your lower back down into the floor and gently tilt your pelvis so that the pubic bone rises, then tilt it back down.

3 Repeat several times, using a slow, steady rhythm.

Leg slide

Another easy exercise for tightening your stomach muscles.

1 Lie on your back with your knees bent, your feet flat on the floor, and your arms by your sides, palms facing the floor. You can put a flat pillow or towel under your neck for support, if you like.

2 Tighten your abdominal muscles by gently pulling in your navel towards your backbone.

3 Gently tilt your pelvis so that the pelvic bone rises.

4 Raising the toes of one foot, breathe out while sliding your leg forwards as far as it will go, with your heel on the floor.

5 Hold for a count of three, then return to the starting position and repeat using the other leg.

Lower abdominal raise

This is a harder exercise that will really work your deep abdominal muscles. If it seems easy then you're not doing it properly!

1 Lie on your back with your knees bent, feet flat on the floor and hip-width apart. Make sure your spine is in neutral. Keep your arms by your sides with the palms facing upwards.

2 Lift your legs into the air at an angle of 90 degrees to your body.

3 Tighten your abdominal muscles and slowly lower one foot to the floor then bring it back up again. Repeat this exercise using the other leg.

3

2

These exercises will tone the rectus abdominis muscle, which runs down the front of your stomach. As you lift your head and shoulders, this muscle contracts at both ends. Avoid these exercises if you have neck problems.

WATCH POINT

Never put your hands behind your neck when performing curls as you may tug on your neck muscles and strain your neck vertebrae.

Abdominal curl

Say farewell to sloppy sit-ups – a few properly executed curl-ups will work wonders in helping you achieve a flatter stomach.

1 Lie on your back with a firm, flat pillow or a small towel underneath your head. Keep your feet hip-width apart, parallel and firmly on the floor, and your knees bent. Rest your hands on your thighs.

2 Set your spine to the neutral position and tighten your abdominal muscles. Flex your spine to lift your head and shoulders gently about 30 degrees off the floor. Your hands will slide up towards your knees as you curl. Keep your lower back in contact with the floor at all times. Slowly curl back down in a continuous movement.

To make this harder, put your hands across your chest as you curl. When this becomes easy, you can place your hands at the sides of your head to increase the resistance against which you are working.

Top tips for great curls

- Always keep your knees slightly bent (flexed).
- Breathe out as you curl up and breathe in on the return.
- Never hold your breath when exercising – blood pressure will rise and this can be dangerous.
- Perform all exercises in a slow, controlled manner.
- Don't put your hands behind your neck because you are likely to tug on the neck vertebrae.

Moving curl

This exercise gives your rectus abdominis an intensive workout by repeating the hardest part of the abdominal curl.

1 Lie on your back with your feet flat on the floor, knees bent and your arms by your sides (palms facing downwards). Keep your spine in neutral.

2 Tighten your abdominal muscles. Start curling up by lifting your head and shoulder blades off the floor while reaching forwards with your arms.

3 Curl up about 30 degrees off the floor. Then extend your arms and lift and lower yourself just a few centimetres up and down from this position.

4 Repeat several times, then lower.

OBLIQUE CURLS

Twisting curls work your rectus abdominis muscles and the obliques, the muscles that give definition to the waist. These exercises will tighten your stomach muscles and trim your waist.

Basic oblique curl

1 Lie on your back with your knees bent, feet flat on the floor and hip-width apart. Put your hands by your temples at the sides of your head. Lift your left leg and rest the ankle of that leg across your right thigh – this will turn your supported left leg out slightly. Keep your spine in neutral and tighten your abdominal muscles.

1

2 Curl up, rotating your trunk to the left and breathing out as you do so. Your right elbow should be moving towards your left knee. Keep your left side in contact with the floor to help support your back.

3 Curl back down again, breathing in as you do so.

4 Repeat this exercise to the other side using the other leg.

2

Slightly harder oblique curl

1 Lie on your back with your spine in neutral, your knees bent and your feet flat on the floor, hip-width apart. Put your right hand by your temple at the side of your head. Lift your left leg and rest the ankle of that leg on your right knee. Wrap your left hand around the inside of your left thigh and press your thigh outwards.

2 Breathe in and tighten your abdominal muscles. Breathe out as you curl up and across to bring your right elbow towards your left knee.

3 Curl back down again, breathing in as you do so, then cross over your right leg and work the other side.

Neck support

Many people complain of neck pain when starting abdominal work. This is usually because you are using the neck muscles rather than the abdominal muscles to lift your head and shoulders. One solution is to place a towel behind your head and hold both ends taut so it supports your neck while you are curling up.

WATCH POINT
Avoid this exercise if you have neck problems.

REVERSE CURLS

Reverse curls give a good workout to the transversus abdominis, the deepest abdominal muscle that wraps around your waist like a corset, and the rectus abdominis, the stomach muscle that's responsible for the six-pack look.

Reverse curl

Remember not to arch your back as you do this exercise.

1 Lie on your back with your spine in neutral, your arms by your sides, palms facing downwards. Tuck your knees in towards your stomach and cross your ankles.

2 Tighten your abdominal muscles by gently pulling your navel in towards your spine.

3 Roll your knees towards your chest and then lower them down again.

WATCH POINT
Remember to breathe regularly throughout.

How muscles work

Here's the science: muscles are made up of millions of tiny protein filaments that relax and contract to produce movement. Most muscles are attached to bones by tendons and are consciously controlled by your brain. Electrical signals from the brain travel via nerves to the muscles, causing the cells within the muscle to contract. Movement happens when muscles pull on tendons, which move the bones at the joints. Muscles work in pairs, enabling bones to move in two directions, and most movements require the use of several muscle groups.

Slightly harder reverse curl

1 Lie on your back with your spine in neutral. You can keep your hands by the sides of your head or rest your arms by your sides with the palms facing downwards. Keep your legs up vertically with the knees bent and your ankles crossed over. Tighten your abdominal muscles.

2 Tilt your pelvis forwards so that your bottom lifts off the floor, keeping your legs still as you do so. Lower your pelvis to the start position.

Ditch the sit-ups

Never do full sit-ups – curling is much safer and more effective. To exercise a muscle properly, it has to be worked as a prime mover – in other words, the main muscle that contracts to move a joint. In a sit-up, the abdominals are the prime movers for only the first 30 degrees of movement, after which the remainder of the movement relies on the hip flexor muscles, which are attached to the lower back. Since this is not a rigid attachment point but a flexible column, strong tension in the hip flexor muscles can put enormous strain on your lower back.

2

CHALLENGING CURLS

Your stomach muscles will work really hard with these exercises but they're not for absolute beginners. You should wait until you've toned your abdominal muscles with a few weeks' worth of routines before you attempt these exercises.

Side reach

The small, controlled movements in this exercise work your stomach muscles even harder.

1 Lie on your back with your spine in neutral, your knees bent, feet flat on the floor, hip-width apart, and palms down and by your sides. Tighten your abdominal muscles.

2 Lift your head and shoulders off the floor to an angle of 30 degrees. Hold this position and reach out with your right hand towards your right calf.

3 Gently move back and forth ten times, then curl back down again. Remember to breathe regularly throughout.

4 Now repeat this exercise, reaching out with the left hand towards the left calf. Gradually build up the number of reaches you can do.

4

2

Long-arm curl

You will need to be able to perform basic curls with ease before you attempt this.

1 Lie on your back with your spine in neutral, your knees bent, feet hip-width apart and flat on the floor. Raise both arms above your head.

2 Engage your abdominal muscles, and begin to slowly curl your head and shoulders off the floor. Keep your arms in line with your ears throughout.

3 Continue the movement using your abdominal muscles, until your upper back is raised at an angle of 30 degrees.

4 Hold for a count of two then slowly lower yourself back down, breathing in as you do so.

'Hundreds'

This is a Pilates exercise – a system of exercise much favoured by dancers – that tones the whole abdominal area. For a harder version, lift your legs off the floor and extend them (still keeping your knees slightly bent).

1 Lie on your back with your hands by your sides, hovering above the ground, palms facing downwards. Keep your knees slightly bent and your feet on the floor throughout. Your spine should be in neutral. Tighten your abdominal muscles.

2 Curl your head and shoulders off the floor but keep your lower back in contact with the floor throughout. In this position, move your arms up and down, slowly breathing in and out as you do so. Breathe in for five flaps and out for five.

Double-leg push-out

This exercise works the transverse (deep) abdominal muscles as you extend your legs.

1 Sit on the floor with your knees bent and your feet parallel, toes just touching the floor but your heels lifted off it.

2 Lean back slightly and support yourself by placing your hands behind you, palms downwards. Tighten your abdominal muscles.

3 Extend both legs in front of you but do not straighten your legs completely. Bring them back to the starting position.

Dressing for a flatter stomach

Find practical solutions to help you look your best and feel positive about the way you look right now. Don't try to hide your lumps and bumps under baggy tops and elastic-waisted jogging bottoms – this just draws attention to the fact that you've got something to hide! Buy clothes that fit properly: stomach-skimming vests really don't look nice on fuller figures. Finally, keep high heels for special occasions only. Heels throw your body weight forwards, ruining your posture.

Leg kick-up

This is a tough one and only for when you can perform curls with ease.

1 Lie on your back with your spine in neutral and your arms stretched out behind your head. Bend your right knee and keep your right foot flat on the floor but keep your left leg extended a little with the knee slightly bent.

2 Tighten your abdominal muscles by gently pulling your navel in towards your spine. Slowly curl your shoulders off the floor and bring your left leg up towards your chest, raising your arms as you lift. Release down to the floor and repeat on the other side.

Keeping up your motivation

All too often people start a new exercise regime burning with enthusiasm, only for it to peter out very quickly to the point when they can't be bothered to do anything at all. When you start your toning programme, be realistic about how and when you can do it. You do need to set aside a regular slot for your 6-minute routine so it becomes a natural and automatic part of your everyday routine, just like brushing your teeth. But if you do miss several days, don't get disheartened and give up – a little exercise even on a very irregular basis is still better than nothing at all!

WATCH POINT
Make sure you keep your chin off your chest.

1

2

WATCH POINT
Don't do this exercise
if you have back problems.

Pillow roll

This exercise tones and strengthens your obliques and is a safe way to mobilize your spine. Your shoulders and arms should stay on the floor throughout but you may find to begin with that the opposite arm and shoulder come up slightly.

1 Lie on your back on the floor with your arms out to the sides at shoulder height, palms flat on the floor. Keep your knees bent. Your feet should be touching and off the floor but to make this exercise easier you can keep your feet on the floor throughout if necessary.

2 Put a cushion or pillow between your knees – this will make you keep your knees together, which is important for this exercise.

3 Tighten your abdominal muscles and remember to breathe normally – do not hold your breath.

4 Slowly bend your legs towards the floor on your right side, rolling your head to the left. Feel each part of your body peel up as you move – your buttocks, then hips, then waist and ribs. Keep going until your right knee and foot are touching the floor with your left leg lying on top.

5 Move your knees and head back to the central position.

6 Repeat this exercise on the other side with your legs towards the left side and your head to the right.

Toe touch

This exercise helps to flatten the deep transverse muscles.

1 Lie on your back on the floor with your spine in neutral, your knees over your hips and your feet raised, parallel to the floor.

2 Tighten your abdominal muscles by gently pulling in your navel towards your backbone – do not suck in your waist or hold your breath.

3 Slowly lower one leg until your toes touch the floor. Move your leg back to the starting position, then repeat on the other side.

Bin the broom handle

A long-practised exercise is to place a pole or broom handle across your shoulders and, with your arms stretched along it, twist your body vigorously from side to side in the hope that this will help to whittle your waist. This sort of exercise actually does more harm than good because it produces a ballistic twisting movement around the spine (the axis of rotation). Not only are you likely to damage your obliques, you may also stretch and tear tiny spinal ligaments. In addition, the weight of your upper body pressing down exerts extreme force on your spinal column.

CHALLENGING CURLS

Leg lift

This exercise helps to develop the deep (transverse) abdominal muscles as well as working your hamstrings (the muscles at the back of your thighs).

1 Lie on your back with your arms by your sides, palms facing downwards. Keep your knees bent and feet hip-width apart, flat on the floor. Tighten your abdominal muscles.

2 Raise your left leg to the ceiling, keeping your knee slightly bent, then lower it. Then raise your right leg and lower it in the same way.

Setting the pace

It's important to work at the right intensity if you're toning up – put in too little effort and you won't notice much difference; throw yourself into the exercises and you may hurt yourself. The aim of a toning programme is to make your muscles work harder, either by increasing the time you exercise or by increasing the intensity of your workout. Your muscles will start to become tired during the last repetitions and you may feel a burning sensation in the area you're working but this is normal and will pass as soon as you rest. Muscle soreness and stiffness is highly likely in the beginning, particularly if you're new to exercise, but if you can hardly move then you've overdone it. Rest up for a day or so and start again at a reduced intensity.

2

Leg stretch

This exercise tests your balance as well as working your stomach muscles.

1 Lie on your back on the floor with your feet hip-width apart and your knees bent. Breathe in to prepare.

2 As you breathe out, tighten your abdominal muscles and pull one knee at a time up to your chest.

3 Breathe in and grasp your left knee with both hands.

4 Breathe out and slowly straighten your right leg up to the ceiling, keeping your back and your shoulders on the floor at all times.

5 Breathe in and bend the right leg back into your chest. Repeat the exercise with the other leg.

WATCH POINT
If you feel your back arching, raise your extended leg higher to flatten it out.

MORE OBLIQUES

Both these exercises are great waist-whittlers but you may find them too hard if you're a beginner – you should be able to do these after a few weeks of stomach-toning exercise.

Side lift

This exercise works the obliques and reinforces your body's natural alignment. Make sure you don't use the supporting arm to push yourself up – the movement is controlled by the stomach muscles.

1 Lie on your side in a straight line. Extend your lower arm above your head in line with your body. Bend your top arm in front to support you – your hand should be in line with your chest.

2 Tighten your abdominal muscles, then lift both legs together off the floor.

3 Now raise your upper leg higher, keeping it parallel with the bottom leg.

4 Hold for a count of two then lower the top leg to the bottom leg.

5 Lower both legs slowly to the floor. Repeat on the other side of your body.

Don't rest too much
Don't stop for more than a minute between exercises. Shorter recovery periods result in better muscles all round and improved muscle endurance. Keep it up!

WATCH POINT
Don't arch your back.

Repetitions

Muscle-building exercises are done as a series of repetitions. One repetition equals one exercise. A set is a group of repetitions and usually consists of anything between 6 and 12 repetitions. To build strength and endurance you will be asked to repeat the same exercise again and again. The aim is to work until your muscles feel tired, and over time this will strengthen them so that they can work harder.

Bicycle

This is a tough exercise that really works the obliques – and you'll need strong abdominal muscles to do this exercise properly. Make sure your shoulders are off the floor throughout.

1 Lie on your back with your knees bent and your hands cradling the sides of your head for support.

2 Tighten your abdominal muscles and curl up about 30 degrees off the floor.

3 Slowly bring your right knee to your chest. Straighten your left leg out without letting it touch the floor.

4 Drop your right leg and repeat with your left leg.

To make this exercise even harder, as you bring your knee to your chest, twist your torso towards your knee so that the opposite elbow touches it.

WATCH POINT
Don't bring your elbows together – keep them open.

STRETCHES

Your exercise routine concentrates on working your abdominal muscles hard to shorten them but it's important to remember that these muscles also need to be stretched in order to keep your body supple and injury-free.

Cobra stretch

This modified yoga position is excellent for stretching your stomach muscles.

1 Lie on your front on the floor and put your hands underneath your shoulders.

2 Breathe in to prepare, then gently push your arms up until they are straight but your elbows are not locked. This will lift your head and chest upwards and you will feel a stretch in your abdominal muscles. Your hips should stay in contact with the floor throughout.

3 Hold for a count of ten then lower yourself back to the ground.

WATCH POINT
Stretch only as far as is comfortable otherwise you may strain your back muscles.

Lying waist stretch

1 Lie on the floor on your back with your knees bent and your feet flat on the floor. Keep your arms stretched out to either side. Breathe in to prepare.

2 Breathe out and pull in your abdominal muscles. Slowly bend both knees to the left while turning your head to the right.

3 Hold for a count of ten then return to the starting position. Repeat, bending your knees to the other side.

Sitting body twister

1 Sit on the floor with your legs straight out in front of you. Bend your left leg and cross it over your right knee.

2 Gently rotate your trunk and head towards your right as far as is comfortable, keeping your buttocks on the floor throughout.

3 Hold for a count of ten then release and return to the starting position. Repeat on the other side.

WATCH POINT
Stretch only as far as is comfortable.

Side stretch

1 Kneel on your left knee and straighten your right leg out to the side.

2 Put your left hand on the floor and bring your right arm over your head until you feel a stretch in your side.

3 Hold for a count of ten then return to the starting position. Repeat on the other side of the body.

Top tips for super stretching

- Only stretch warm muscles.
- Slowly ease the muscle into position.
- Do not bounce into position.
- Never overstretch – mild discomfort is acceptable but if it hurts, you should stop.
- Don't hold your breath – breathing freely will enable blood to flow to the muscles.

2

Standing waist stretch

1 Stand with your legs fairly wide apart, knees soft. Turn your right foot outwards and bend the knee of the right leg so that you can lunge to that side. Keep your left leg straight with the foot flat on the floor and pointing forwards. Rest your right palm on your right thigh to support your body weight.

2 Lift your left arm above your head and lean towards your right side. Hold for a count of ten. Repeat on the other side.

1

2

WATCH POINT
Don't lean too far over – you should feel a stretch in your obliques but it shouldn't hurt.

Here's a simple two-week plan for you to follow. Although these exercises are grouped into 6-minute sessions, if you're new to exercise please don't feel you have to start off doing the whole routine — you can build up the amount of time you spend and the types of exercises you do. You can also make up your own routines. The exercises in this book will tone your stomach muscles quickly, but be aware that they are not for fitness or weight loss.

Do what feels right for you

The exercise programme outlined on these pages suggests that you do one 6-minute routine every day. However, if you do not usually exercise regularly it is a good idea to start off by doing the routines every other day to give your body time to recover. Similarly, if you experience stiffness or pain the day after exercising, it is important to take a break that day. Each routine should take 6 minutes to do, but this may vary depending on the amount of reps you do. The workouts gradually build in intensity, so you may wish to repeat the first week's routine in subsequent weeks until you feel ready to incorporate the second week's more challenging schedule into your fortnightly programme.

Day 1

Belly tightener: *2-4 reps* **p126**
Simple pelvic tilt: *1 set (8-12 reps)* **p128**
Abdominal curl: *1 set (6 reps)* **p130**
Pillow roll: *1 set (6 reps) on each side* **p140**
Cobra stretch **p146**
Lying waist stretch **p146**

Day 2

Seated stomach workout: *2-4 reps* **p122**
Seated knee lift: *1 set (6 reps)* **p124**
Hip hitch: *5 reps on each side* **p123**
Easy plank: *2 reps* **p127**
Cobra stretch **p146**
Side stretch **p148**

Day 3

Leg slide: *1 set (10 reps) for each leg* **p128**
Basic oblique curl: *1 set (6-8 reps)* **p132**
Reverse curl: *1 set (6-8 reps)* **p134**
Toe touch: *1 set (6-8 reps)* **p141**
Sitting body twister **p147**
Side stretch **p148**

Day 4

Abdominal curl: *1 set (6-8 reps)* **p130**
Double-leg push-out: *1 set (10 reps)* **p138**
Leg stretch: *1 set (10 reps) on each leg* **p143**
Side lift: *2-4 reps on each side* **p144**
Standing waist stretch **p149**

Day 5

Leg slide: *1 set (10 reps) for each leg* **p128**
Leg lift: *1 set (10 reps) for each leg* **p142**
'Hundreds': *5 reps* **p137**
Side reach: *2 reps on each side* **p136**
Cobra stretch **p146**
Standing waist stretch **p149**

Day 6

Belly tightener: *4 reps* **p126**
Lower abdominal raise:
  1 set (6-8 reps) **p129**
Reverse curl: *1 sel (6-8 reps)* **p134**
Pillow roll: *1 set (6-10 reps)*
  on each side **p140**
Sitting body twister **p147**

Day 7

Easy plank: *2-4 reps* **p127**
Simple pelvic tilt:
  2 sets (16-20 reps) **p128**
Moving curl: *2-4 reps* **p131**
Toe touch:
  1 set (6-8 reps) for each leg **p141**
Leg stretch:
  1 set (10 reps) for each leg **p143**
Cobra stretch **p146**

Day 8

Belly tightener: *4 reps* **p126**

Simple pelvic tilt: *2 sets (16-20 reps)* **p128**

Abdominal curl: *1 set (8-12 reps)* **p130**

Basic oblique curl: *1 set (8-12 reps)*
   on each side **p132**

Lying waist stretch **p146**

Sitting body twister **p147**

Day 10

Belly tightener: *4 reps* **p126**

Moving curl: *1-2 sets (6-20 reps)* **p131**

Long-arm curl: *1 set (6-8 reps)*
   on each side **p137**

'Hundreds': *1 set (6-10 reps)* **p137**

Sitting body twister **p147**

Cobra stretch **p146**

Day 9

Seated stomach workout: *4 reps* **p122**

Seated knee lift: *1 set (6-8 reps)* **p124**

Slightly harder oblique curl:
   1 set (8-10 reps) on each side **p133**

Cobra stretch **p146**

Side stretch **p148**

Day 11

Easy plank: *4 reps* **p127**

Slightly harder reverse curl:
   1-2 sets (10-20 reps) **p135**

Leg kick-up: *1 set (6-10 reps)*
   on each side **p139**

Side lift: *4-6 reps on each side* **p144**

Standing waist stretch **p149**

Side stretch **p148**

Day 12

Lower abdominal raise: *1 set (6-8 reps)* **p129**
Abdominal curl: *2 sets (12-20 reps)* **p130**
Long-arm curl: *1-2 sets (10-20 reps)* **p137**
Bicycle: *1 set (6-10 reps) on each leg* **p145**
Cobra stretch **p146**
Lying waist stretch **p146**

Day 13

Belly tightener *(4 reps)* **p126**
Slightly harder oblique curl:
   1 set (6-10 reps) on each side **p133**
Side reach: *1 set (6-10 reps)*
   on each side **p136**
Leg kick-up: *1 set (10 reps)*
   on each leg **p139**
Sitting body twister **p147**

Taking it further

These routines are fine for toning and sculpting your stomach but if you want to get fit then you'll have to include some activity that raises your heartbeat for at least 15 minutes at a time. Swimming, cycling, fast walking and running are all straightforward options but you could do an exercise class or take up a sport such as tennis if you like – just keep moving and try a variety of activities.

Making the most of your workout

- Always warm up before you begin.
- Think about what you are trying to achieve and be aware of how your body feels as you move.
- Remember to tighten your abdominal muscles.
- Keep your spine in neutral.
- Breathe in to prepare and breathe out as you move into position.
- Move slowly and gracefully.
- Cool down at the end to relax and bring your body back to normal.

Day 14

Moving curl: *1-2 sets (10-20 reps)* **p131**
Reverse curl: *1-2 sets (10-20 reps)* **p134**
Double-leg push-out:
   1-2 sets (10-20 reps) **p138**
Toe touch: *1 set (6-10 reps)*
   on each leg **p141**
Side lift: *1 set (6-8 reps) on each side* **p144**

Working the muscles in your **hips** and **thighs** increases **mobility**, and helps to stabilize and **balance** your pelvis and hip area. Another advantage is that it will make you look **slimmer**.

hips and
thighs

INTRODUCTION

Unless you were born with a figure to rival that of a supermodel, you probably wish your lower half was slimmer and trimmer. The trouble is that hips and thighs are often hard to target – for example, the muscles in your legs are much bigger than those in your arms, so you need to put more effort into getting results.

The benefits

General exercise such as running isn't always effective, so the great thing about this section is that each and every one of the exercises focuses entirely on slimming down and toning up these two trouble zones.

As you can imagine, most involve a lot of leg work and it may take some time for you to build up enough strength in the legs to be able to carry out the series of exercises outlined in the two-week plan, but with practice it will get easier.

Why not take your hip and thigh measurements before you start the plan and again when you finish? Seeing a reduction will spur you on and give you a great sense of achievement.

Effective exercising

Most of these muscle-building exercises are done as a series of repetitions. For exercises that need repeating in order to last for 30 seconds, simply do as many repetitions as you can comfortably achieve in that time. The aim of repeating exercises is to work until your muscles feel tired, and over time this will strengthen them so that they can work even harder. To make it effective, it's important that you don't stop for more than a minute between exercises. Shorter recovery periods result in better muscles all round and improved muscle endurance. So keep going!

The muscles in the hips and thighs

Back of body

BUTTOCKS: there are three buttock muscles – gluteus maximus (the biggest muscle in the body), medius and minimus. They hold your pelvis in position, stabilize your hips and balance the hip area. Buttock muscles help to keep you upright and pull your legs back as you walk. If you spend a lot of time sitting down they're likely to be slack and flabby.

HAMSTRINGS: these are three long muscles below the buttock muscles, which run from the back of the hipbone to the back of the knee. The hamstrings work with the gluteus maximus to bend your knee and rotate your hips.

Front of body

HIP FLEXORS: a group of muscles that run from the hips to the spine and from various points along the thigh bone. They include the adductors (inner thigh muscles) and abductors (outer thigh muscles). They work in opposition to the buttock muscles, helping you to move your hips and lift your thighs and knees.

QUADRICEPS: these are four muscles that run down the front of the thigh. They enable you to extend your legs and bend your hips.

What you'll need

For this section you'll need a non-slip mat or pair of trainers, a chair, two tennis balls, a platform to step up on to or a sturdy bottom stair on a staircase, ankle weights (optional) and a cushion. Don't forget to warm up before you begin and cool down when you finish. Now let's get started.

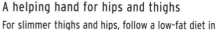

A helping hand for hips and thighs

For slimmer thighs and hips, follow a low-fat diet in addition to your toning and shaping routines.

• Trim all visible fat off meat.

• Steam or grill food rather than frying or boiling.

• Fill up with carbohydrates that release their energy slowly – for example, wholegrain pasta, rice and cereals.

• Eat plenty of fresh fruit and vegetables.

• Drink plenty of water. This will flush out toxins from your body that can cause the appearance of dimpled flesh on your thighs.

POSTURE

Practise these easy exercises to improve your posture. Remember to keep your movements smooth and flowing throughout.

1

4

Backside tilt

This simple exercise works your hip extensors (gluteus maximus) and is essential for good posture.

1 Stand up straight with your feet hip-width apart and your knees slightly bent. Rest your hands on the top of your hips.

2 Tighten your abdominal muscles by gently pulling in your navel towards your spine – don't suck in your waist or hold your breath.

3 Slowly tilt your pelvis forwards then return to the starting position. The movement should come from your buttocks.

4 Slowly tilt your pelvis backwards then return to the starting position.

Up and down

This is a good exercise for strengthening the quadriceps and for improving your body's alignment. You'll need two small balls for this exercise – tennis balls are ideal.

1 Stand behind a chair and place one ball between your ankles. Place the other ball between your legs just above your knees. Hold on to the chair to keep your balance.

2 Stand up straight with good posture. Slowly rise up on your toes.

3 Slowly come back down again. When your heels are on the floor, gently bend your knees, keeping your heels on the ground. Slowly move up into the starting position.

How to stand properly

Good posture looks relaxed and natural, not hunched or slouched. Stand with your feet hip-width apart. Gently pull up through your legs, keeping your knees slightly bent. Lengthen your spine, pull in your stomach muscles and stand tall. Keep your shoulders down and relaxed so that your neck is as long as possible, and make sure that your weight is distributed evenly over both feet.

WATCH POINT
Don't bend forwards or backwards as you bend your knees.

STANDING EXERCISES 1

If you only ever do one type of hip and thigh exercise, make it a squat, which really hits the spot! Squats work the hip extensors, hamstrings (back of thigh muscles) and quadriceps (front of thigh muscles). Tight quads and hamstrings cause poor posture and lower back pain so it's very important to keep them in good working order.

Basic squat

Targeting the buttocks and tops of the thighs, this easy exercise is great for toning up those trouble spots. Remember to keep your knees soft (slightly bent) throughout.

1 Stand up with good posture, your feet hip-width apart and your hands on your hips.

2 Tighten your abdominal muscles by gently pulling your navel towards your spine.

3 Bend your knees and squat as if you were going to sit down. Only squat as far as is comfortable and without losing your balance.

4 Return to the standing position by pushing through your heels, keeping your knees slightly bent as you do so.

3

4

Wide squat

Wide squats are great for toning your inner thigh muscles and the front and back of the thighs. Try not to wobble.

1 Stand up with good posture, your feet wide apart and your toes turned out. Keep your hands on your hips.

2 Tighten your abdominal muscles by gently pulling your navel towards your spine.

3 Bend your knees and lower your bottom as if you were going to sit down.

4 Go as low as you can without wobbling forwards. Return to a standing position by pushing through your heels, keeping your knees slightly bent as you do so.

Single-leg squat

This slightly harder squat really challenges your balance as well as working your hips and thigh muscles.

2

1 Standing with your feet together and your arms by your sides, shift your weight on to your right foot. Rest the toes of your left foot next to your right foot for balance.

2 Keeping your back straight, bend at the hips and knees and slowly sit back on to your right leg, raising your arms in front of you as you lower. Sit back only as far as is comfortable. Stop and hold for a count of two.

3 Now press into your right foot through the heels and come back up.

4 Repeat the exercise with the weight on your left foot.

WATCH POINT
Keep your abdominal
muscles tight
throughout these
exercises.

Lunges are fantastic for firming your hips and thighs, because they work the hip extensors, quadriceps and hamstrings. They're also good exercises to help you improve your balance. When you have become adept at performing lunges, you could hold weights in each hand to increase the workout and you could even do walking lunges, as long as your workout space is big enough, or you are able to turn mid-stride.

Basic lunge

This is a fabulous hip and thigh toner that is extremely versatile because you can hold it for increasing amounts of time. Keep your back straight at all times and keep your movements smooth and fluid.

1 Stand up straight with good posture and your hands on your hips. Tighten your abdominal muscles by gently drawing your navel towards your spine, and tense your buttock muscles.

2 Take a big step forwards. Your back leg should be long and slightly bent at the knee, with the heel off the floor; the front leg should have the knee over the ankle.

3 Dip your lower body down as far as is comfortable. Hold for a count of two.

4 Push your body all the way back up to the standing position using your front leg. Do all your repetitions on one leg then switch legs and repeat on the other side.

WATCH POINT
Don't lunge too deeply – if you let your knee go beyond the line of the end of your toes you will put too much stress on your knee joint.

3

Platform lunge

This is a modified lunge that is great for sculpting the thighs and bottom for a longer, leaner look.

1 Stand up straight with your hands on your hips. Tighten your abdominal muscles to protect your back, and tense your buttock muscles.

2 Take a big step forwards on to a 15–30 cm (6–12 inches) platform. Your back leg should be long and slightly bent at the knee, with the heel off the floor; the front leg should have the knee over the ankle.

3 Dip your lower body down as far as is comfortable.

4 Push back with your front leg to return to a standing position. Do all your repetitions on one leg then switch legs and repeat on the other side.

WATCH POINT
Leaning forwards on the way down puts strain on your back and may cause loss of balance.

Even if you're office-bound for a large part of the day or spend a lot of time travelling, you can still sneak in a few exercises to keep your hips and thigh muscles toned. You'll need a straight-backed, sturdy chair for these exercises – not one on castors.

Seated leg extension

This easy exercise is great for toning the quadriceps, the muscles at the front of your thighs. To make this harder, you can use ankle weights to strengthen the intensity of the exercise.

1 Sit up straight with good posture. Tighten your abdominal muscles by pulling in your navel towards your spine – this will protect your back muscles.

2 Press your knees together and straighten one leg. Hold and release. Do all your repetitions on one leg, then repeat on the other leg.

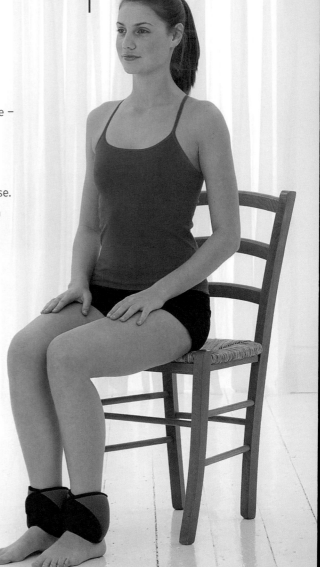

Making the effort

It's important to work at the right intensity if you're aiming to tone up your muscles – if you work out until it hurts you may damage your muscles; put in too little effort and you won't notice any difference. Your muscles should start to become tired during the last repetitions and you may feel a burning sensation, but this is normal and will pass as soon as you rest. Muscle soreness and stiffness is highly likely in the beginning, but if you can hardly move then you've overdone it. Rest up for a day or so and start again at a reduced intensity.

Simple seated thigh squeeze

This tones and strengthens your inner thighs. Make this exercise harder by increasing the time of the squeeze and by using something with more resistance, such as a semi-inflated ball.

1 Sit up straight on a chair with your knees bent and feet together.

2 Place a cushion between your thighs. Squeeze the cushion as hard as possible for a count of five, then release.

As well as tightening up your gluteals, these bridging exercises will help to stabilize your pelvis and your trunk muscles, and work your hamstrings. Take care not to over-arch your back or let it sag, and remember to keep your breathing steady and controlled throughout.

Stability bridge

You need to perfect this exercise in order to improve the stability of the trunk muscles before you can move on to more challenging movements.

1 Lie on your back with your knees bent and your feet flat on the floor, slightly apart. Keep your arms by your sides, palms facing downwards.

2 Tighten your abdominal muscles by gently drawing in your navel towards your spine (which will support your back).

3 Press your lower back down into the floor and gently tilt your pelvis forwards so that the pubic bone rises.

4 Use your hip, thigh and trunk muscles to lift your pelvis until your body forms a straight line from your shoulders to your knees. Hold for a count of five then return to the starting position.

4

2

Bridge squeeze

This buttock-clenching exercise makes the gluteus maximus work to support your back. If you feel a strong contraction in your hamstrings or any strain in your lower back, then you are not using your buttock muscles properly.

1 Lie on your back with your knees bent and feet slightly apart.

2 Tighten your abdominal muscles by gently drawing in your navel towards your spine – (which will protect your back muscles).

3 Curl your bottom off the floor, lifting your pelvis until your knees, hips and chest are in line.

4 Hold this for a count of ten, squeezing your buttock muscles to support the bridge position. Release and repeat.

Types of movement

You will come across the following terms in this book:

ABDUCTION: when you move away from the centre of your body, for example, by raising your leg horizontally in Lateral leg raises.

ADDUCTION: when you move towards the centre of your body, for example, by lowering your leg horizontally in Lateral leg raises.

EXTENSION: straightens a limb or the spine.

FLEXION: bends a limb or the spine.

ROTATION: when your body turns on its axis.

3

Bridge with leg lift

Lifting one leg strengthens the muscles at the back of the buttocks and thighs while increasing balance and control in your stabilizing muscles.

1 Lie on your back with your knees bent and feet slightly apart, and your arms at your sides.

2 Tighten your abdominal muscles by gently drawing in your navel towards your spine.

3 Curl your bottom off the floor, lifting your pelvis until your knees, hips and chest are in line.

4 Extend one leg, lift it level with the knee then lower to the floor. Do all your repetitions on one leg, then repeat on the other leg.

To make this exercise harder, raise your extended leg towards the ceiling, then fold the knee towards your chest and lower your leg back to the starting position. You could also use ankle weights.

Controlling your movements

Make sure that all exercises are performed slowly, carefully, and with your full attention. You really do need to concentrate on what you're doing and think about how your body is responding to any exercise. If an action hurts or you do it too quickly then you're not doing it properly. Movements should flow in a gentle, controlled manner. This enables your muscles to stretch naturally.

4

One-legged buttock clencher

This is a harder exercise that will really work your gluteals.

1 Lie on your back with your knees bent and your feet flat on the floor, slightly apart. Keep your arms by your sides, palms facing downwards.

2 Place your left foot on to your right knee. Tighten your abdominal muscles to support your back.

3 Press your lower back down into the floor and gently tilt your pelvis forwards so that the pubic bone rises. Lift your hips off the floor and squeeze your buttock muscles, then release.

4 Do all your repetitions on one leg then repeat on the other leg.

Buttock walking

This exercise is brilliant for keeping your bottom trim and strengthening the buttock muscles. The floor is a good option because a hard surface is more taxing, but beware of carpet burn, or splinters from old wooden floors.

1 Sit up straight with your legs stretched out in front of you. Cross your arms so that your hands are resting on your shoulders.

2 Breathe in and lengthen your spine. Breathe out, and breathe normally as you 'walk' forwards on your buttocks – ten steps forwards, ten steps back to form one repetition. Repeat as often as you can.

WATCH POINT
Take care not to over-arch your back.

STANDING EXERCISES 2

As well as exercising your hip and thigh muscles, these leg lifts help to improve your balance. You will need to hold on to the back of a chair or a table for support for all these exercises. Keep movements smooth and fluid and move only as far as is comfortable.

Lateral leg raise

This exercise helps to tone and tighten your outer thigh muscles and your hips, as well as improve your balance.

1 Stand up straight with good posture, hands by your sides and feet together, holding on to the back of a chair with both hands for balance.

2 Tighten your abdominal muscles by gently drawing in your navel towards your spine. This will protect your lower back muscles.

3 Raise one leg out to the side about 45 degrees. Keep your toes pointing forwards and hold for a count of three. Relax and do all your repetitions on one leg, then repeat using the other leg.

WATCH POINT
Keep your body straight and both knees soft throughout.

Front leg raise

This exercise strengthens and tones the front of your thighs (quadriceps) and increases your hip flexibility. It also helps with your balance.

1 Stand up straight with your feet together and hold on to the back of a chair sideways with your left hand to balance. Tighten your stomach muscles.

2 With your left leg slightly bent, raise your right leg out in front of you as far as is comfortable. Hold for a count of three.

3 Lower your leg, then do all your repetitions on that leg. Repeat on the other leg.

Rear leg raise

This strengthens and tones the buttocks, lower back, back of hips and hamstrings. It also helps with your balance. For best results, keep your buttocks tensed throughout – it's harder but better for you in the long run.

1 Stand up straight with your feet together and use your right hand to hold on to the back of a chair sideways to help you balance.

2 Pull in your stomach muscles to support your back and tighten your buttock muscles.

3 Take your right leg back, and touch the floor with your toes. Hold this position for a count of three, then return to the start. Do all your repetitions on one leg, then repeat on the other leg.

These traditional ballet exercises give a great workout to the legs and buttocks. Keep your movements controlled and flowing.

Double knee bends

This exercise, which strengthens your thighs, calves and buttocks, will help you achieve the sculpted legs of a dancer.

1 Stand with your legs a little wider than shoulder-width apart and your feet slightly turned out. Rest your hands on the back of a chair to help you balance.

2 Tighten your abdominal muscles to protect your lower back.

3 Slowly press your knees out and lower yourself down. You should feel this in your bottom and back of your thighs.

4 Return to standing, then tense your buttocks, squeeze your inner thigh muscles and rise up on to your toes. Return to the start position.

One-legged knee bends

These will strengthen your buttocks, thigh muscles and calves.

1 Stand up with good posture with your right side to the back of a chair and hold on to it for support. Lift and bend your right leg backwards so that the knee faces forwards and your foot is pointing out behind you in line with your knee.

2 Tighten your abdominal muscles to protect your back.

3 Slowly rise up on to the toes of your left foot. Hold for a count of two.

4 Slowly come back down again on to your left foot.

5 Now bend your left knee, bringing the kneecap directly over your foot.

6 Straighten up and repeat five times on the same leg, then do this exercise on the other leg.

Quality control

Focus on perfecting your technique – it's the quality of the movements that will count. Remember to keep your spine aligned and your abdominal muscles pulled in at all times.

3

WATCH POINT
Don't let your bottom stick out.

5

Try these lying-down exercises to work on your thighs and hips. Remember to keep your movements smooth and flowing throughout, and breathe regularly.

Lying kick

This works the hips, bottom and leg muscles.

1 Lie on your left side and bend your left leg beneath you. Support your head with your left hand and put your right hand on the floor in front of you.

2 Tighten your stomach muscles to protect your back and keep your spine in neutral.

3 Slowly bring your right knee up to hip level then slowly push the right leg out straight (but not so that the knee locks). Bend the leg back.

4 Do all your repetitions on one leg then repeat on the other leg.

3

3

Lying inner thigh lift

This is a good one for toning and shaping inner thigh muscles, but don't stretch your legs so wide that your muscles hurt.

1 Lie on your back with your legs straight up in the air.

2 Keep your spine in neutral and tighten your abdominal muscles.

3 Pull your legs out to the sides so that they form a 'V' shape – you will feel a stretch in your inner thigh muscles.

4 Bring your legs together back to the start position.

3

WATCH POINT

Make sure your spine is in the right position when you are exercising. If you exercise with your pelvis and spine misplaced – either pressed too far into the floor or arched – you may put stress on your lower back and create muscle imbalance.

Scissors

This exercise is fabulous for toning your inner thighs and your stomach muscles.

1 Lie on your back with your legs straight up in the air. Keep your spine in neutral and tighten your abdominal muscles to protect your back.

2 Make a 'V' shape with your legs and then, in a smooth, continuous motion, cross your left leg in front of your right leg, then switch sides in a scissor-like motion.

2

FLOOR EXERCISES 2

Exercising on all fours makes your muscles work harder because they're working against gravity. Keep all movements smooth and controlled for best results and don't let your back sag or arch.

Leg lift

This is a lateral thigh raise that works the outer thigh muscles (hip abductors).

1 To start, kneel in the 'box' position (on all fours) and keep your back straight. Tighten your abdominal muscles to support your back.

2 Lift your right leg out to the side – you will feel the muscles at the side of the thigh and hip working to lift your leg. Hold for a count of two.

3 Slowly lower your leg to the start position. Do all your repetitions on one leg, then repeat using the other leg.

Don't exercise if...

- You are feeling unwell – your body will need all its strength to fight off any infection.
- You have an injury – you might make things worse.
- You have an ongoing medical condition or are on medication – consult with your doctor first.
- You've just had a big meal.
- You've been drinking alcohol.

One-hip leg extension

This exercise works the hip extensors (gluteals). To increase the intensity of this exercise, straighten out the leg you are working (but keep the knee soft).

1 Get into the box position and keep your back straight.

2 Tighten your abdominal muscles to protect your back. Tense your buttocks.

3 Lift your right leg upwards with your knee bent and your thigh parallel to the floor.

4 Gently lift your thigh about 5 cm (2 inches) up and then lower again. Lower the leg back to the floor then do all your repetitions on one leg. Repeat the exercise with the other leg.

WATCH POINT
Don't kick back vigorously because this builds up momentum, which can place stress on your lower back muscles.

Kneeling kick-back

This works your quadriceps.

1 Get down on all fours and pull in your stomach muscles to protect your back.

2 Raise your right leg off the floor, and with your knee bent, bring it into your body, then stretch it out backwards so that it is in line with your body with the foot flexed.

3 Pull the leg back in and take it back out again. Do all your repetitions on one leg, then repeat using the other leg.

These side-lying exercises work the abductor muscles at the side of the thighs. Remember to keep your back straight, your hips facing forwards, and breathe regularly throughout.

Outer thigh lift

Make sure you perform each move slowly and in a controlled way to really work the muscles. You don't have to tense your buttocks as you do this but it's good to work your gluteals whenever you can.

1 Lie on your right side with your body in a straight line and your thighs and feet together. Prop yourself up with your right arm and rest your left hand on the floor in front of you. Tighten your stomach muscles by drawing your navel in towards your spine – this will help to protect your back.

2 Bend both knees. Lift up the top leg, then lower, squeezing your buttocks together as you raise and lower your leg.

3 Do all your repetitions on one side then repeat them on the other side of your body.

WATCH POINT
Keep the knee of the extended leg
soft (slightly bent).

2

Straight-legged outer thigh lift

1 Lie on your side with your lower leg bent and your top leg straight but with the knee soft rather than locked. Your body should be in a straight line and your thighs and knees together. Prop yourself up on your elbow with your head resting on your hand and place the other hand in front of you for support. Keep your stomach muscles pulled in to protect your back.

2 Raise your top leg then lower, squeezing your buttock muscles as you do so. If you are in the correct position you shouldn't be able to lift your leg more than 45 degrees.

3 Do all your repetitions on one side then repeat them on the other side of your body.

Keeping up your motivation

All too often people start a new exercise regime burning with enthusiasm, only for it to peter out very quickly to the point where they can't be bothered to do anything at all. When you start your toning programme, be realistic about how and when you can do it. You need to set aside a regular slot for your 6-minute routine so it becomes a natural and automatic part of your everyday routine. But if you do miss several days, don't get disheartened and give up – a little exercise even on a very irregular basis is still better than nothing at all.

These side-lying exercises work your inner thigh muscles (abductors). Remember to keep your spine in neutral and your stomach muscles tightened throughout.

Inner thigh lift

1 Lie on one side with your hips facing forwards and your body in a straight line. Prop yourself up on your elbow with your head resting on your hand and place the other hand on the floor in front of you for support.

2 Tighten your stomach muscles by gently drawing in your navel towards your spine to protect your back.

3 Bend your top leg so that the knee touches the floor in front of you.

4 Raise the bottom extended leg, keeping the knee soft (slightly bent), then lower.

5 Do all your repetitions on one side then repeat them on the other side of your body.

1

4

Straight-legged inner thigh lift

This is a harder exercise, which tones your
inner thigh muscles.

1 Lie on your side with your hips facing
forwards and your body in a straight line.
Prop yourself up on your elbow with your
head resting on your hand and place the
other hand on the floor in front of you
for support.

2 Tighten your stomach muscles by
gently drawing in your navel towards
your spine to protect your back.

3 Bend your top leg and place the foot
flat on the floor just above the knee of
the extended leg.

4 Raise your extended leg off the floor
as far as you can (this won't be very
far) then lower.

5 Do all your repetitions on one side
then repeat on the other leg.

Working with your body shape

We all have a unique bone structure and body shape
that, frankly, we can't change. Some of us are
genetically programmed to be very slender
(ectomorphs), others are curvaceous with a tendency
to gain weight (endomorphs), while others tend to be
athletic (mesomorphs). It's important to work out the
shape you are before embarking on your fitness
routine – if you are a natural endomorph, no amount
of exercise or dieting will give you a waif-like,
ectomorphic look. Furthermore, women are naturally
designed to store fat on the hips and thighs to
protect the reproductive organs – that is, until the
menopause, after which they will store fat around
the midsection, just like men!

WATCH POINT
Don't raise your bottom leg too high
– you'll over-extend the muscles.

4

Stretching relieves the muscle tension that is created by exercise and allows the muscles to relax to their full length. This ensures that their full range is used and they do not remain in a semi-contracted state. Stretches help to develop flexibility and keep your body supple and injury-free, and you can perform these at the end of your session, when your muscles are well warmed up.

Lying buttock stretch

This will stretch your buttocks and your outside thigh muscles.

1 Lie on your back and bend your legs. Cross your right ankle over your left knee and lift your left leg off the floor. You will feel a stretch on the outside thigh and buttock of your left leg.

2 Take hold of your left thigh with both hands and slowly draw the left knee in towards you. You will feel the stretch intensify.

3 Hold the stretch for a count of ten. Release and repeat on the other leg.

1

2

Lying quad stretch

1 Lie prone (face down) on the floor. Bend one knee and take hold of the foot of that leg with your hand and gently pull the foot towards your buttock.

2 Press your hip down towards the floor (which will ensure you stretch fully the rectus femoris – the quadriceps muscle that crosses the hip joint).

3 Hold the stretch for a count of ten, then release and repeat on the other leg.

2

Lying hamstring stretch

1 Lie on your back with your knees bent and your feet resting flat on the floor.

2 Lift one leg and grasp the back of the thigh with your hands.

3 Gently pull that leg towards your chest as far as is comfortable. Repeat on the other leg.

3

STRETCHES

Sitting inner thigh stretch

It is very important to stretch the inner thigh (adductor) muscles because they help the quadriceps and hip flexors during running.

1 Sit on the floor with your knees bent and the soles of the feet together, keeping your back straight. Rest your hands on your inner thighs, just above your knees.

2 Use your arms to press downwards to abduct the hip joints and thus stretch the inner thigh muscles as far as is comfortable. Hold for a count of 20, then release.

2

3

Sitting outer thigh stretch

1 Sit on the floor with your legs stretched out. Cross the left leg over the right leg, with the left foot flat on the floor on the outer side of the right knee.

2 Rest your left hand on the floor behind your body, with your arm straight to support your upper body.

3 With your right hand, pull your left knee gently over to the right.

4 Hold for a count of ten and feel the stretch in the top of the outer left hip region, then release. Repeat the exercise on the other side.

Standing hip flexor stretch

You can keep your back knee on the floor for this exercise if you find it difficult to keep your leg straight.

1 Kneel on your right leg, keeping your left leg bent and your left foot firmly on the floor.

2 Put your hands on the floor either side of your left foot to help you balance.

3 Lift your right knee off the floor and straighten the right leg backwards (keeping the knee soft). Dip your pelvis down to the floor as far as is comfortable.

4 Hold for a count of ten, then release and repeat on the other leg.

3

TWO-WEEK PLAN

Here's a simple fortnightly routine for you to follow. Although these are broken down into 6-minute routines, if you're new to exercise don't feel you have to start off doing the whole routine – you can build up the amount of time you spend and the types of exercises you do. You can also make up your own routines. The exercises in this book will tone your hip and thigh muscles within a few weeks but please be aware that they are not for fitness or weight loss.

14-day schedule

The routines below will give your abdominal muscles a good workout. Each routine should take 6 minutes to do, although this may vary depending on the amount of repetitions you do – don't worry if you can't do the full amount at first. The routines also take into account the time it will take for you to get into position and have a short rest between each exercise.

Day 1

Backside tilt: *1 set (6–8 reps)* **p158**
Basic squat: *1 set (8–12 reps)* **p160**
Front leg raise:
    1 set (8–12 reps) for each leg **p171**
Rear leg raise:
    1 set (8–12 reps) for each leg **p171**
Double knee bends: *1 set (8–12 reps)* **p172**
Lying buttock stretch **p182**
Lying quad stretch **p183**
Lying hamstring stretch **p183**

Day 2

Seated leg extension:
    1 set (6 reps) for each leg **p164**
Simple seated thigh squeeze:
    1 set (6 reps) **p165**
Stability bridge: *(2–4 reps)* **p166**
Bridge with leg lift:
    1 set (6–8 reps) for each leg **p168**
Lying kick: *1 set (6–8 reps) for each leg* **p174**
Lying buttock stretch **p182**
Sitting inner thigh stretch **p184**

Day 3

Up and down: *1 set (6–10 reps)* **p159**
Buttock walking: *1 set (8–12 reps)* **p169**
Outer thigh lift:
   1 set (6–8 reps) for each leg **p178**
Inner thigh lift: *1 set (6–8 reps) for each leg* **p180**
Lying buttock stretch **p182**
Sitting inner thigh stretch **p184**
Sitting outer thigh stretch **p185**

Day 4

Basic lunge:
   1 set (6–8 reps) for each leg **p162**
Lateral leg raise:
   1 set (10 reps) for each leg **p170**
Front leg raise:
   1 set (8–12 reps) for each leg **p171**
Rear leg raise:
   1 set (8–12 reps) for each leg **p171**
One-legged knee bends:
   1 set (6–8 reps) for each leg **p173**
Lying buttock stretch **p182**
Lying quad stretch **p183**
Lying hamstring stretch **p183**

Day 5

Bridge squeeze: *1 set (6–8 reps)* **p167**
Bridge with leg lift:
   1 set (6–8 reps) for each leg **p168**
Lying kick: *1 set (8–10 reps) for each leg* **p174**
Scissors: *1 set* **p175**
Lying buttock stretch **p182**
Sitting inner thigh stretch **p184**
Standing hip flexor stretch **p185**

Day 6

Up and down: *1–2 sets (8–12 reps)* **p159**
Basic squat: *1–2 sets (8–16 reps)* **p160**
Lateral leg raise:
   1–2 sets (10–20 reps) for each leg **p170**
Front leg raise:
   1–2 sets (10–20 reps) for each leg **p171**
Rear leg raise:
   1–2 sets (10–20 reps) for each leg **p171**
Lying buttock stretch **p182**
Lying quad stretch **p183**
Lying hamstring stretch **p183**

Day 7

Backside tilt: *1–2 sets (10–20 reps)* **p158**
Platform lunge:
   1–2 sets (6–12 rep) for each leg **p163**
One-legged knee bends:
   1 set (6–10 reps) for each leg **p173**
Outer thigh lift:
   1 set (6–10 reps) for each leg **p178**
Inner thigh lift:
   1 set (6–10 reps) for each leg **p180**
Lying buttock stretch **p182**
Sitting inner thigh stretch **p184**
Sitting outer thigh stretch **p185**
Standing hip flexor stretch **p185**

TWO-WEEK PLAN

Day 8

Up and down: *1–2 sets (8–16 reps)* **p159**

Wide squat: *1 set (8–12 reps)* **p161**

Front leg raise:
1 set (8–12 reps) for each leg **p171**

Rear leg raise:
1 set (8–12 reps) for each leg **p171**

One-legged knee bends:
1 set (8–12 reps) for each leg **p173**

Lying buttock stretch **p182**

Lying quad stretch **p183**

Lying hamstring stretch **p183**

Day 9

Seated leg extension:
1–2 sets (10–20 reps) for each leg **p164**

Simple seated thigh squeeze:
1–2 sets (6–12 reps) **p165**

Stability bridge: *1 set (6–10 reps)* **p166**

Bridge with leg lift:
1 set (6–10 reps) for each leg **p168**

One-legged buttock clencher:
1 set (6–10 reps) for each leg **p169**

Lying buttock stretch **p182**

Sitting inner thigh stretch **p184**

Day 10

Buttock walking: *1 set (8–12 reps)* **p169**

One-hip leg extension:
1 set (6–8 reps) for each leg **p177**

Straight-legged outer thigh lift:
1 set (6–8 reps) for each leg **p179**

Straight-legged inner thigh lift:
1 set (6–8 reps) for each leg **p181**

Lying buttock stretch **p182**

Sitting inner thigh stretch **p184**

Sitting outer thigh stretch **p185**

Day 11

Platform lunge:
1–2 sets (10–20 reps) for each leg **p163**
Lateral leg raise:
1–2 sets (10–20 reps) for each leg **p170**
Front leg raise:
1–2 sets (10–20 reps) for each leg **p171**
Rear leg raise:
1–2 sets (10–20 reps) for each leg **p171**
One-legged knee bends:
1 set (6–8 reps) for each leg **p173**
Lying buttock stretch **p182**
Lying quad stretch **p183**
Lying hamstring stretch **p183**

Day 12

Bridge squeeze: *1 set (6–8 reps)* **p167**
Bridge with leg lift:
1–2 sets (8–16 reps) for each leg **p168**
One-legged knee bends:
1–2 sets (8–16 reps) for each leg **p173**
Scissors: *2 sets (16–20 reps)* **p175**
Lying buttock stretch **p182**
Sitting inner thigh stretch **p184**
Standing hip flexor stretch **p185**

Day 13

Single-leg squat:
1–2 sets (8–16 reps) for each leg **p161**
Lateral leg raise:
1–2 sets (10–20 reps) for each leg **p170**
Front leg raise:
1–2 sets (10–20 reps) for each leg **p171**
Rear leg raise:
1–2 sets (10–20 reps) for each leg **p171**
Double knee bends:
1–2 sets (6–12 reps) **p172**
Lying buttock stretch **p182**
Lying quad stretch **p183**
Lying hamstring stretch **p183**

Day 14

Up and down: *1–2 sets (10–20 reps)* **p159**
Platform lunge:
1–2 sets (8–16) for each leg **p163**
One-legged knee bends:
1 set (6–10 reps) for each leg **p173**
Straight-legged outer thigh lift:
1 set (6–10 reps) for each leg **p179**
Straight-legged inner thigh lift:
1 set (6–10 reps) for each leg **p181**
Lying buttock stretch **p182**
Sitting inner thigh stretch **p184**
Standing hip flexor stretch **p185**

INDEX